MEMORIES OF
A CATHOLIC
BOYHOOD

By Harry J. Boyle

THE GREAT CANADIAN NOVEL

STRAWS IN THE WIND

WITH A PINCH OF SIN

A SUMMER BURNING

HOMEBREW AND PATCHES

MOSTLY IN CLOVER

MEMORIES OF
A CATHOLIC
BOYHOOD

———◆———

HARRY J. BOYLE

1973

DOUBLEDAY CANADA LIMITED, TORONTO, ONTARIO

DOUBLEDAY & COMPANY, INC., GARDEN CITY, NEW YORK

Library of Congress Catalog Card Number 73–79648
ISBN: 0-385-08003-4
Copyright © 1973 by Harry J. Boyle
Printed in the United States of America
First Edition

CONTENTS

MEMORIES OF
A CATHOLIC
BOYHOOD

Chapter 1

GRADUATION

———◆———

A country boy of the 1920s was a creature of his environment. He adjusted to the seasons as easily as the natural, free creatures of the fields and forests. Winter was cold and he dressed for skating and sleigh-riding. Spring was sensual and lazy. In summer he shed clothes to the point of censure from his mother and managed a great deal of daydreaming, fun, and frolic in spite of his father's attempts to press-gang him into work.

Fall took the barefooted lad into the confining atmosphere of a one-room school, which should have dampened his spirits. It did, but only slightly. The bare wooden structure was a circus of many rings, presided over by a pale young woman. She dispensed fundamental education and worried over glimpses of flesh or underwear that might arouse the lust lurking in the eyes of older boys.

Two facts were apparent. She taught school as a stopgap until some young farmer would propose marriage, and if too much time elapsed she would accept an older bachelor, or failing that, a widower. The students by and large didn't expect to go beyond their high school entrance examinations, or if they failed, the mandatory sixteenth birthday when they could drop out and start farming in the tradition of their fathers.

Separate school students had an advantage over public school

ones. The Catholics had holidays on holy days as prescribed by
the Church. But in return they had an admixture of catechism
every day and a Friday afternoon grilling on matters of faith by
the parish priest. On the first Friday of each school month, after
confession on Thursday afternoon, they were expected to attend
Mass and receive Communion.

Girls studied. Boys did a minimum of studying. A boy who was
precocious or dared to suggest that he enjoyed school had to
compensate by an interest in sports or indulgence in pranks.
Passing my entrance examination at eleven along with a trio of
rawboned lads of fifteen and sixteen was an ordeal. It was slight
compared to the trauma of going away to the neighboring town
of Bingham to enter high school.

I went because my parents, unlike most of the others in that
western Ontario valley, saw education as a way of qualifying me
for a better life. I was naïve and young. My only salvation was a
physique that compared favorably with that of my fifteen- and
sixteen-year-old companions. Because I was so young high school
became a confining period of self-discovery. It was shackling compared to the romping free times of early life.

Because the high school in Bingham was a public one, my years
there marked an interruption of the daily catechism and weekly
inquisition of a Catholic education; but as I was to learn, in the
plans of my mother at least, this was to be only a temporary pause.

The high school days seemed interminable at first. Seven students lived at McCann's rooming house; we inhabited the odd-
shaped upstairs rooms and the vast, dark kitchen of the T-shaped
house for three years. We were country-bred, and if our early
school days were the light, then the high school days were
the shadow which had to pass before we felt the liberation of graduation.

It arrived, and I will always remember the Thursday eve of that
graduation exercise. Being fifteen years old at this time wasn't as
difficult as being eleven at entrance had been. For one thing, the
students there had much less prejudice against education than the

boys of the one-room country school. Some high school students even had ambitions; town lads tended to follow their fathers as druggists, doctors, or some kind of professional. A lot of the town girls admitted that university would provide a broader hunting ground for husbands than Bingham afforded. My country counterparts were mostly confused about their future, except for one lad who was determined to be a veterinarian.

"You know," he observed as we walked out of class for the last time, "there's only eleven of us Catholics here and we have the toughest time of all. Catholic mothers push their boys to be priests and the girls to be nuns. I have a Protestant father who wants me to be a cattle buyer like himself and my mother has a fool idea I should be a Christian Brother like her cousin. I suppose I have it worse than even the rest of you. Maybe I could be a holy vet who buys cattle for a monastery."

He stopped my snicker.

"You'll laugh differently when your mother starts pushing you into a seminary."

I protested, but there was a cold prickliness on my spine. It only left when I began speculating about how on Friday, the white-bricked building, turned gray by age, would have a garland of bunting across the skinny throat of the tower over the main doors. Already, the gymnasium was precisely dotted with hard chairs, and the sawhorses borrowed from Maclone's mill held planks for a platform to accommodate the officials. Everyone knew that the principal would make a speech sprinkled with the same jokes that everyone had read in copies of the *Police Gazette* at Allan's barbershop. But, teetering on the edge of tipsiness, he would go ahead and deliver them. Anyway, there was a certain curiosity about his ability to remember the clean version.

That evening I lay on my cot, suffering the internal distress of a communal fried dinner of odds and ends that had been intended as a farewell feast. Fortunately, Joe McAllister had been restrained from adding a pint of his mother's chili sauce. It had patches of mold and aural evidence of fermentation, but Joe was Scotch and loath to waste it.

As usual, Sue-Bell Phillips was monopolizing the bathroom. As usual, the running taps failed to drown the sounds of her nightly straining against the bonds of constipation.

Ted, my dormouse-like roommate was crouched by a mirror, stalking his favorite prey, blackheads. Soon he would lurk in the hall for another futile encounter with Laura. Laura was an agile minx who wore a carefully adjusted housecoat that was calculated to induce what I suppose was frustrated lust in all of the boys. But now Ted was the only one who regarded accosting Laura as anything more than a ritual.

"Tonight, I'm really going to find out. Tonight."

The dormouse was pear-shaped. His constantly erupting face and the straggling hairs of a developing beard gave him a perpetual appearance of decomposition.

"Ted, you've been trying to corner her for three years. What chance is there tonight?"

He panted the answer, sweeping his hands over his belt buckle.

"Laura asked me to come in and help with her trunk. Boy, her housecoat was down to here—"

Ted existed on jam, peanut butter, cookies, and bread, all of which he kept stored in a box under his bed. He was full of sexual fantasies, read all the racy books he could beg, borrow, or steal, and ate in bed at night. Our room was never really clean, so to come awake at night and hear munching sounds meant having to determine whether it was a convention of grateful mice or simply Ted stuffing himself, or both.

I was packed. My one suit was gray, a matter of some concern to me since someone had told me that blue was mandatory for a platform appearance. When I asked my father about this one weekend near graduation, he said impatiently, "Boy, don't you know what year this is? It's 1931."

Now the suit pants were between newspapers, being firmed into what I hoped would be some form of a press by the squeeze of mattress on springs.

"What are you going to do when you go home, Ted?"

He paused with arms akimbo and fingers poised against a prominent pimple, thought for a moment, and then triumphantly squeezed an eruption.

"I don't know. Clerk in my uncle's grist mill, I guess. He ain't very good on figures. Say, did I ever tell you about the girl in the office?"

"Yes, you did. All about her."

He shrugged his shoulders and went back to pursuing pimples.

It was a dreary room, the wallpaper patterned with bilious green garlands of what must originally have been designed as ivy. Two boxy wooden beds, two rickety cots, an overhead trio of three bells of glass which never had more than two working forty-watt bulbs, and board contraptions on each side of the door covered by faded chintz curtains for clothes storage made up the furnishings.

There was one window between the heads of our beds. My roommate and I tolerated each other; but the one point of dissension was the window. He kept closing it. I opened it to counteract his pervasive smell. He was inclined to wear his clothes in a permanent way, even to bed, compensating—during his fruitless pursuits of Laura—by dousing himself with Florida water.

"I'm going out."

I had to get out. The walls were coming in, and the ivy garlands on the wallpaper threatened to choke me. I creaked down the back stairs, our official entrance, and across the greasy kitchen illuminated only by the porch light filtering through the dusty curtains.

Outside there was the lingering radiance of daytime, but the street lamps were increasing their pools of light as day faded. It was a soft June night of murmuring sounds and the brisk swish-swash of the sprinklers up the street around the undertaker's castle of a house.

Miss Emily was isolated in the parlor of the front, lower half of the house as if determined to pretend that the McCanns were still well-to-do. She probably rationalized the seven mad roomers in the remainder of the house as servants. We only met her to pay the rent. It was a ritual. On Sunday evening when you returned from a weekend at home with your food for the week, you stowed it in your cupboard in the kitchen. Then you walked through the vacant passageway once said to have been a butler's pantry and rapped on the door.

"Who is that, please?"

"It's Harry."

"Just a moment."

Bolts slid. A key turned. The door opened a fraction to disclose a tiny woman, wearing an elaborate lace shawl. There was a rank smell, not unlike the one you get when a rotting plank is lifted in a stable. Birds screeched and cats poked angry faces through at her feet with menacing yowls.

"Yes."

It was the tone of a person being bothered, and it discouraged conversation. It was suggestive of how monarchs might deal with subjects. Her hair was thin, like raveled white yarn over a pink scalp, and her face was a vague silhouette without features except for the outline of gold-rimmed spectacles that glinted and disguised her eyes.

"The room money."

She accepted the dollar and fifty cents in her bird-bony hand, muttered unidentifiable words of dismissal, and closed the door with the dungeon sounds of locks and bolts. She lived with her cats and innumerable cages of canaries. Sometimes if you were alone in the kitchen, you could hear muffled screeching and yowling.

On this night, I could see that she was sitting again in the rocker by the bay window. I would leave the next day, not knowing any more about her than when I arrived. I would never know if it was true that she buried her dead canaries at night among the wild roses and lilacs of the once elegant garden, or kept them, as my roommate suggested, rolled in old newspaper among the family silver and linen.

The story was that she had been an attractive, reserved girl living with her widowed father, Captain Tom McCann. He left town in company with the young wife of a neurotic, evangelist preacher. Miss Emily then simply closed herself from the world, dismissing the servants and managing to survive by renting rooms to high school students. She ignored them as she ignored the town.

Bingham!

I had lived for three years in Bingham without knowing the place. There was the farm from Friday night to Sunday night and all during summer vacation, and the remainder of the time I simply went to high school. In town I felt gauche and awkward. The country was my milieu but now that it was time to leave I had disturbing thoughts.

I had wanted to go to high school in Handrich, the lake town and county seat.

"Why can't I go to Handrich?"

My reasons for going on to high school were vague. It was based more on a craving to read than on any desire to acquire an education, but Handrich harbor was a magnet of long lakers, a sandy beach, a railroad yard, blue water stretching to the U.S.A. and to a place called Michigan and, of course, a carnival atmosphere.

"No, I think Bingham has a very good school. It will be better for you than Handrich. That's what I have been told."

The skin tightened on my mother's chin and the chords of her neck. It was a sign that she was teetering on the edge of truth. She would probably be admitting it on Saturday night in the confessional cubicle. But it was something to be justified, because my cousin, Mike, ran away at fourteen to ship on a lake freighter as a cabin boy. There was something about sailors and exposure to sin in Handrich, which she feared in a remote way. Sailors obviously had a hard time gaining the kingdom of heaven.

Like the other country boys and girls, I had moved from the

comforting warmth of home to exposure in this place of 1,386 people where the straight Main Street began on a swampy flat and ran a half mile to where the railroad station and the creamery stood on the banks of the Maitland River. The town spread out on either side, running up the hillside on one side of the high school and the hospital. On the other, it stretched to the edge of the bending river. On the further side of that arm, there was the fairground (used once a year) and the makeshift homes of the people who made a meager living as unskilled workers in an assortment of glove factories and small industries. Each year, the Maitland River flooded this lower town. It seemed like a deliberate attempt to flush the place out of the consciousness of those who lived in the more affluent atmosphere of Bingham proper, which was on high ground.

The country students had an affinity for the ones from lower town. They were marked because their elders were constantly appearing in the weekly magistrate's court in the faded green council room down the corridor from the public library in the town hall. The charges were bootlegging, or trapping out of season, occasionally chicken stealing, and common-law squabbles. This happened uptown as well, but there it was labeled politely as trouble between a man and his housekeeper.

Our sun-reddened necks and hands marked *us* as strangers. The girls were conscious of dresses with drooping hems and misplaced waists put together by mothers with more zeal than fashion sense. The boys sensed that their wrists and hands dangling from short sleeves and the outlines of rangy legs in puckered pants caused amusement.

The town wasn't sophisticated. Just the same, it had more life in it on an average day than our local village of Clover could muster on a summer Saturday night. Town-bred students were articulate, where we were inclined to gaggle and redden in the face if a teacher seemed amused. Our training called for formal respect for all elders. Town pupils were flippant, and dismissed lack of

knowledge with a shake of the shoulders. We were mortified by
not knowing an answer.

There was an invisible line of separation. School dances did little to break down the wall. Most of us could stomp, wheel, and
fake our way through a square dance, but our feet had a habit of
getting cork-screwed into panicky positions in the subtleties of
the fox trot, especially if we were rash enough to try talking to our
partners. After such an experience even the most democratic town
girl was inclined either to hide in the ladies' room or to murmur,
"Sorry, this dance is taken."

We were hopeless at cadet drill. In our scratching khaki suits
we resembled a bunch of sausages in loose skins, bumping and
straggling along. Up to this point, marching, for farm boys, had
been the irregular drill of following a walking plow in a furrow or
stumbling behind a harrow cart. We didn't seem to have qualifi-
cations for either the gymnasium floor or the packed dirt of the
parade square. One bellow from the physical training instructor
with a remark such as, "Look, you clumsy plow jockeys, keep in
step," was enough to eliminate all traces of co-ordination. We con-
soled ourselves with fantasies of the wooden simulated rifles
magically becoming lethal weapons with which to reduce the P.T.
instructor to a heap of quivering flesh.

A few of us developed certain scholastic talents, but we did have
resilience in sports. Most townies had only to collide with the
solid, work-hardened body of a country boy a few times to realize
that discretion was the better part of valor. Sneaky players found
it perilous to get squeezed between two Concession characters
when a referee was distracted.

At first, we accepted the fact that we were outsiders. In time
we realized there were others forced to remain beyond the invisible pale around the insiders of school life. Some worked harder,
as we played harder, hoping, I suppose, for acceptance.

Florence was a light, coppery-colored girl whose father was a
full-blooded Indian pensioner from the Great War, unable to
work after being gassed at the Somme. Her white mother worked

as a chambermaid in a hotel. Florence was beautiful and walked with a stunning grace. She kept her dignity as she passed groups of town boys who threw suggestive and derisive remarks in her direction. Older town boys drove slowly by her small house in lower town on Saturday nights, but respected the fact that her father had been a sniper.

Tom Ham had a smiling, yellow face. His father and mother worked in a tiny, steamy building doing laundry which Tommy delivered after school. He ran the gauntlet of snobbery. There was a mob temptation to taunt him for being Oriental. Some, no doubt, were jealous of his proficiency in mathematics.

Others were marked by having parents who didn't conform in the smug little town. Betty Henry was an undernourished girl with a passion for art. Something came alive in this creature, who looked like a perpetual scarecrow in sloppy, hand-me-down dresses, when she applied pen, pencil, or brush to paper in drawing or art class. The point of the instrument would fly, making tracks that added up to a picture, startling in beauty or realism. We slopped and copied and tried to ignore her talent, as if it couldn't be housed in such a person. Talent was associated in our minds with the beautiful and the privileged.

Betty Henry bore a cross that was neither color nor race. Her father was a tough, self-educated product of the London slums who preached for better wages and working conditions at a time when men tried to make themselves believe that having a job under any condition was a privilege. He survived simply because no one was better at his trade. Betty carried the cross for his fierce crusading.

Sammy was a lean and lanky boy with soulful eyes that protruded in a face hardened by something we sensed as unusual for a child. He was dogged and determined. In oral composition, he was magical. His voice, after you became accustomed to the cadence, produced an almost musical effect. What Sammy had was experience. His soul had been seared somewhere, but he remembered only the good memories in his compositions, and he took us into the close and crowded quarters of a European ghetto. We felt the dangers that had made his father a refugee down the hidden roads. If we had been more aware of the outside world, we would have learned, long before anyone else, what was due to explode in that faraway Europe of his birth.

Sammy's father was a bent man who had a bargain store off Main Street. Our parents went there to buy when money was scarce. His father's accent was so thick that at times Sammy would have to uncoil himself from reading and come to act as interpreter. With the carelessness of youth, we imagined that there must be justification for the harassments reported in the local paper from fire inspectors and town officials. We never thought for a moment that he represented any threat for the big stores on Main Street so solidly established by the fathers and grandfathers of the current owners.

We lost some of our gaucherie in the poolroom, but played largely by ourselves at the back table. In the silence of the library, presided over by a gentle, white-haired woman, there was mutual interest in books. We had bittersweet pangs of love for town girls who ignored us. We felt loneliness on soft days for the smell of growing things on country hillsides and dreamed impossible dreams of what would come when school was over.

I walked the streets of Bingham that night and heard porch voices and crickets. A whistle blew at the foundry for a shift change and I imagined the hot steel snapping and spitting as it was poured from the ladles into the sand molds. There was a clattering, rackety sound up on the third floor of a building where tired men and women sewed gloves by machines. Students packed the soda fountain but I couldn't force myself to go in and be casually but deliberately ignored.

Bert, the night constable, clicked the latches of the stores.

"Finished tomorrow, eh?"

"Yeah, it will be all over."

He thumped his flashlight in his free hand.

"I envy you. God, I wish I had never left the farm."

He was gone then. Three businessmen came out the back door of the haberdashery and swept by, stumbling slightly as they got into a car and drove partway down Main Street without lights until Bert gave them a series of warning flicks with his flashlight. I started to walk up and wait for the late train from Toronto, but decided against it. There was too much loneliness about the train, pausing and then swooshing off again on its journey in the mysterious night.

On the way to McCann's, the giggling and scuffling sounds from the bushes at the edge of the public school grounds disturbed me. Ted was in bed, mumbling about the dire things Laura deserved. She had not only discouraged him but had described in detail how repulsive she felt him to be. I lay awake most of the night and listened while he ate.

The front rows of chairs were filled next day with the same kind of people we saw at the Armistice Day ceremonies at the Cenotaph. There were at least fourteen clergymen, representing the town's amazing diversity of Christianity. They clustered, except for the Anglican and Roman Catholic, who were bound by the tie of having been padres in the war. Both were either praised or damned because it was known that they met secretly and "drank."

My father, like most country parents, sat at the back. People were expectant because there were to be awards. The school orchestra played lustily, although with difficulty because of the variation between the movements of Miss Luscombe's Adam's apple and her baton. The chairman of the school board took over the ceremonies after the principal told his old jokes, while the teachers huddled at one end of the platform. They looked sheepish, in contrast to their normal attitude of command. The country pupils were delighted when a township boy was given an award for shopwork. His entry was a beautiful set of book ends, carved from seasoned wood and polished to perfection. The award was assumed since the principal had already asked for them, without mentioning compensation.

Then the blows came. The pale daughter of a mill owner was given the prize for poetry; a councilman's undistinguished son received one for mathematics; a daub of flowers from the lawyer's daughter took the art award . . . and on it went! We sat stunned, and when it was over the principal stood up and coughed and said, "Thank you very much" and left the stage before the anthem was sung, clutching the book ends.

On the drive home I was silent.

"Cat got your tongue?"

It poured out then about Tom, Betty, and Sammy and the unfairness of it all. My father listened and didn't comment. He called attention to grain fields, envied a new windmill, and even stopped to look at some Hereford steers grazing. When we came to the gate he idled the Model T.

"Just remember one thing. Someday you'll be proud you knew the ones you cared about. For the most part, they'll make it. But those others—you won't even be able to remember them, let alone be bothered by them. Listen, son, you've started on a trip. The last three years are just the first step. Where it's going, I don't know."

He pushed his foot on the clutch pedal and started to move the gas lever with his hand and chuckled.

"I will say one thing. You've got one good thing going for you. I'm glad you're on the side of those youngsters and not toadying up to the others."

Snap was barking as we drove up the lane of elms to where my mother stood on the back veranda drying her hands on her apron.

Chapter 2

KISSING COUSIN

It was 1931.

I came home from high school unaware of what was going on in the world and assuming there was another pleasant summer ahead. It was never to be the same. I had changed. For that matter, the world had begun an inexorable change—one that hasn't stopped yet.

This was the year when half a million people were out of work in Canada. Magistrates, in desperation, were seeking a wider use of the lash. The League of Nations said "no" to a Chinese plea for investigation, while approving Japan's promise to promote peace in Manchuria. H. G. Wells was urging the need for a world dictator. We didn't know or really care about all this because the countryside and the village of Clover bore little relationship to what Marshall McLuhan today calls the "total electronic environment." Our environment was scarcely even mechanical, because the horse collar was still vital. Hard times were not such a visible factor as you might imagine. People didn't mind saying, "We can't afford it." Collectively they felt they were lucky to live in the country.

My uncle, who operated a crossroads grocery store, visited more often than usual and my mother was suspicious.

"What did Johnny want?"

She had a deathly fear of business. The farm was a secure place, and my father was a farmer. He should stick with it. Uncle John's problem, as retold by Father, was simple: "The wholesalers are pressing him for money and he can't get any cash out of his customers. He's caught in the middle. Besides, I don't think he was cut out for business."

Mother frowned. "He should have stayed on the farm. That's where all of us should stay."

Father caught the hint and relapsed into silence. He didn't seem convinced. Women were all alike because they felt secure when their husbands stayed on the farm. Anything could happen in business. But Father was beginning to despair about farming. Grandfather changed the subject, or tried to, and made matters worse.

"Joe Cammen is back from Detroit. Got laid off at the Ford plant. Don't know how he can expect his brother to look after him."

Mother used the news to her advantage.

"Business again. You see what I mean. At least a person has enough to eat on the farm. You remember how they lorded it over us when they first went to Detroit. New cars and new clothes. They really thought we were stick-in-the-muds."

Bill Cammen took his brother and his family in, and they put one car up on blocks and started using the other one. By that fall, they would take the wheels and body of the car, put a floor on it and hitch it to a team of horses. This was the local equivalent of what western farmers were calling "Bennett Buggies," after the Conservative Prime Minister, R. B. Bennett.

At first, there seemed no place in the world to compare with our back stoop at the beginning of the summer.

Farmers, after the turn of the century, were anxious to display success and get rid of memories of log houses or small, frame buildings constructed by barn carpenters. So they built enormous houses of brick or stone and disregarded the inadequacy of wood stoves to combat winter cold in rooms with extra high ceilings.

Front hallways were like station waiting rooms and from late November to mid-April they had sub-Arctic temperatures.

They darkened the houses by putting wainscoting around each room, decorating them with combs and rollers in what was vainly called graining. Wallpaper had dark flowers against brooding backgrounds. Large rooms with small windows added to the feeling of gloomy medieval castles.

The eaves were decorated with curlicues and doodads. Some had stained glass in the casement around the front door. And each had to have an enormous front veranda facing the roadway. Sometimes there was a balcony on top of the veranda, but they often forgot to put in a doorway to the upper hallway. Even if they did put a door in, it remained shut, with a table covered with ornamental ferns jammed against it on the inside. The front veranda was a never-used mark of success.

The focal point of family activities during the summer was the back stoop! It was built of leftover lumber and was really only a platform with a roof supported by several skinny scantlings. Blocks served as steps. The floor was usually far enough from the ground for a small boy or dog to crawl under.

The back stoop had a rocker, with a few light slats tacked across to help hold it together. It required a cushion unless you didn't mind painful seating. A couch with the springs peeking through was covered by a moth-eaten buffalo robe. A homemade bench was shoved against the side wall of the kitchen.

A small oilcloth-covered table was crowded with house plants that had been moved from the kitchen as soon as the danger of frost passed. The outside window sill was covered with items picked up in the yard which people didn't know what to do with. There was, for instance, a doorknob, a badly rusted key, a broken wrench, a paperweight which had once provided a mock snowstorm when agitated but which had lost its power to snow, a hammer head waiting in vain for a new handle, several worn files, some harness buckles, and so on . . .

Mother queried the value of the assortment every time she swept the back stoop.

"Now, I'll take them down to the driving shed in the morning," answered Father, but the pile was never moved.

The back stoop was a place to sit. You could listen to the sounds of the countryside in the summer. Across the river you might hear a man talking, without being able to distinguish the words. Mother kept busy with her hands, shelling peas or snapping the ends from beans just picked from the garden. The evening came down imperceptibly, and the bats would swoosh out from their daytime sleeping places in the eaves and the bugs would butt uselessly against the screen door if the lamp was lit in the kitchen.

"Sure is peaceful."

"Be hot tomorrow," Grandfather would forecast, taking into account the way the sun had set and the small night breezes coming up the gully.

The talk was light and gentle. Father and the hired man were letting tiredness from the day's work ooze out of their systems. Grandfather nursed his pipe, the smoke aromatic on the night air. Finally, someone yawned and it was contagious. Soon, we were all yawning and when Father stood up and stretched himself, it was a signal to go to bed, and no one argued the decision.

This was the easy, casual life of our valley. It was also the life of our nearest village, Clover. Everyone knew his place, and woe betide the stranger who came along to upset the even tenor of the village ways.

Clover wasn't a very big place. It had practically everything a person wanted except legal liquor, but that was supplied illegally. There was a proliferation of churches of all kinds, with Continuing Methodist and Continuing Presbyterian defiantly added after Church Union. A group of revivalists, who set up in a vacant store and did their baptizing in the Maitland River in warm weather, supplied variety in the religious line.

There were three general stores, a harness shop, a feed, flour, and seed store, Medd's Tailor Shop, Lee's Café, and so on. It was a typical Ontario village, and if you happened to ask for some item that was not in stock, it was a simple matter for the merchant to have it sent in next day on the city train.

The acme of gourmet satisfaction in the village was a five-cent ice cream cone from Lee's Café, which started dripping almost as soon as you had it in your hand. It was cherished down to the soggy tip.

Green apples produced uncomfortable results almost every year. On the other hand, nothing compared with the taste of the first Astrakhans when they colored and reached the point of dark seeds. There was a pilgrimage to be made to the grass farm for small wild apples that had a tang of their own. We also managed several trips to the wild raspberry patches that grew in profusion on slashes where the bush had been cut down and where tree trimmings remained.

Hard times and all, the country rang with fun. There were garden parties and dances. Older people complained that they didn't know how young people could go to dances and do their work, comfortably forgetting earlier boasts about their own prowess in getting along so well on so little sleep in the busy season.

There was excitement! At least one barn in the district used to be sacrificed to fire each year. Experience never seemed to teach some people the folly of storing green hay or wet sheaves. If the spontaneous combustion that can result from that didn't do it, there was lightning. A man who felt he couldn't afford lightning rods could be the poorer for economy.

There was tragedy, too. A man might be killed with a runaway team. Others were maimed by machinery, because this was the time when the country was moving over to mechanization. Many men without mechanical skill or experience were making their initial contact with the dangerous complication of the new equipment.

We got really hot weather in late July. The ponds dried up and the swale grew into itself, with the outer edges becoming firm underfoot.

Village boys pedaled by on their bicycles looking for fruit trees to rob. Their idleness seemed to be almost sinful in the face of so much activity in the country. College students, that year, walked down country roads willing to trade magazine subscriptions for a minimum of cash or something to eat.

Days merged into nights and nights into days in an almost hypnotic way. I didn't look at a calendar, as if the time might stretch magically when you didn't consult the figures.

Yet, I must have sensed some significant things that summer. My family stopped pressing me to work. Farmer schoolmates from the local school were distant. There were sly references to the books I borrowed and read from the little library in the village.

"All that reading will make your head soft."

I had touched and been touched by the words of prose and poetry. I was in that breath-catching time when emotions were forming too rapidly to be really enjoyed. There was a world beyond our valley, and there were relationships to be formed with people outside of the family circle. Girls, something to be avoided like the plague during early school days, now had a magnetism that was hard to resist.

Parents called the stage "mooning." It was an apt description in many ways, because suddenly the night had a greater attraction than the day. From being a day creature, romping and playing and soaking up every minute and moment of the daylight, I found a new attraction in the night.

Half in and half out of parental discipline because I had been away, I chose to find excuses to stay out in the night. There was always a chore to do, an errand to run, or a conference that became vitally important.

"I have to check something with George. I won't be long."

"Why didn't you think of it earlier?"

"I just got to it."

"What about tomorrow morning?"

"Oh, I won't have time."

Reluctantly, the permission came:

"Well, but don't be too late now."

The approach to the Higgins' place was a challenge. Like an Indian scout, I had to sneak past the pond, under a dip in the line fence, and then, keeping in the gully, wait until I saw George. The other children would be "peekabooing" on the lawn. Our signal was a sharp whistle, then a pause, and then a small yelp like a pup.

"Shhh. Paw thinks I'm in bed."

We moved back down the gully and up along the line fence to the road. We had to be careful but the precautions were part of the fun. Soon we came to the Fitzgerald place. I suppose there's a Fitzgerald family in every community. They were carefree and happy and lived with an amazing lack of discipline. Mrs. Fitzgerald was a stout woman with fiery red hair that always seemed to be spiraling off into disorderly twists she kept brushing back from her forehead.

"Them two fellas are here again."

I winced every time her laughter and voice boomed out, notifying the two girls. It seemed our parents a half mile away would hear it. Ella and May materialized shadowlike behind the screen door and giggled. A few years before, such a pair of girls would have sent us packing, but this time we persevered.

"Who's out there?"

"It's us."

"Who's us?"

"Aw, go on."

Soon we were romping around the lawns, coming finally to sit exhausted on the front veranda. It seems strange now to remember that the two girls were so much more glamorous and attractive in the evening than in the daytime.

May giggled the most. Ella was the one who liked poetry. Presently, the moon would appear and, while May teased George, Ella would lean back against the veranda post and recite. It gave me goose pimples to hear her.

"And all my days are trances,
And all my nightly dreams
Are where the dark eye glances,
And where the footstep gleams;
In what ethereal dances,
By what eternal streams!"

How I remember that poem! Once she copied it for me and I carried it secure in the bib pocket of my overalls. When we had to leave we were jealous because the girls could stay out on the porch. The Fitzgerald home was our concept of an untidy Eden.

I slipped up quietly and sat at the edge of the back stoop. Father and Grandfather talked in hushed voices and inside Mother read or worked by the light of the lamp on the table. The night was filled with the gentle sounds of wild creatures.

"Where is that boy?"

"I'm here."

The idea was to pretend, without saying so, that you had been there for some time.

"You better go to bed or you'll never get up in time."

Sometimes one of them would ask in what seemed to be an amused way, "How's George?"

It was years before I learned they knew all about the excursions to the Fitzgerald house.

We considered Handrich, the county town, a part of the mysterious, outside land. It was a lake port with summer hotels where city people, mostly from Buffalo, came up to sit on the verandas. Some ventured onto the sandy beach or played at the mysterious game of golf on a new course laid out on the flats where the river took a meandering and lazy S-turn before emptying, reluctantly, into the harbor.

While the pace of the older visitors was slow and relaxed, their families were more active. They whizzed around in automobiles, played tennis, sailed small boats out of the harbor, flocked to the ice cream parlors and restaurants, and made a hangout of Hong's Café. The young men wore ice cream pants of cream flannel with colorful blazers, smoked cigarettes, and patronized Haig's Billiard Parlor, much to the disgust of the regular habitués.

While other lads in the country regarded the world of this kind of summer visitor as an alien world, I looked at it with burning curiosity. The common meeting ground was a dance pavilion on the high bluff overlooking the lake at the edge of Handrich. It was called simply, "The Pav," and the Saturday night dances were a mecca of attraction. Most clergymen in the area preached sermons on the sinful temptations of the institution.

Country parents were inclined to go along with the reverend gentlemen about the dance pavilion.

"It's these city people who go there. You wouldn't know anyone."

"But Ma, Joe Alex has gone and says it's real fun and very quiet."

"Joe Alex! His parents do have a time with him. He even drives the car!"

It was useless to point out that Joe Alex in recent memory, in our own home, had been praised for being industrious because he was working for the summer in the tannery at smelly work. He was also given an accolade for being polite at church because he was one of the few boys in the community who could tip his hat to a lady without seeming self-conscious.

The real rub concerned the Model T. We had progressed to the point where I could drive it to church on Sunday, to the village with the family on Saturday night, or anywhere in case of an emergency. Going to Handrich was different.

Then Joe Alex asked me if I would like to go to "The Pav" on Saturday night. I came home in a state of agitation which almost caused me to drive the car, family and all, over the edge of the creek bridge. I sweated it out on Sunday and finally broke the news to my grandfather Monday morning. He suggested a direct plan of action. Simply say I was going.

I did, and chaos took over. Mother said I was too young to go.

Father was noncommittal. On Thursday, I sprang a new surprise. I was going with a girl. Joe Alex had a date with a girl from Buffalo who was staying with my second cousin. This helped the cause.

"Betty Jean is a nice quiet girl," relented Mother, "and I am sure she would never be a party to rowdiness."

I hadn't seen Betty Jean for some time, but was thankful her name carried so much influence. I polished my oxfords, and wore white pants. They were closer to sailcloth than flannel; but with a blue suit coat taking the place of a blazer and a vivid red tie inherited from a Detroit relative, I was in a gay mood. Mother handed out warnings and many admonitions which Joe Alex accepted with grave politeness. Then she put a parcel on the back seat of the car for my relatives.

We arrived, and I presented the flat parcel which the mother opened to find two leaky raspberry pies. The girl from Buffalo was older than Joe Alex, and Betty Jean, now wearing glasses, proved to be a rather mousey but friendly creature.

We spent the prescribed time in the parlor. After interminable silences punctuated by uncomfortable bits of chat, the father grunted: "You better hurry or the dance will be over." We left immediately. The American girl sat up front with Joe Alex and I sat on the back seat with Betty Jean. There seemed to be moisture on the seat of the car.

The pavilion was somewhat dark when we paid our admissions and went in. I was getting along famously at dancing when, for some reason or other, the lights came on for an announcement from the bandstand. I heard a roar of laughter and someone said: "You're bleeding to death!" The seat of my white trousers was a deep red from what could only have been berry juice.

Youth can't stand much of that kind of thing. I fled. Betty Jean followed me. Trying to be gallant, I suggested that she should go back in, but she offered to have me go home and borrow a pair of her father's trousers. Since he was a railroad engineer of large girth that was hopeless. So we sat and listened to the music, walked to the harbor and came back to a park bench, where she proceeded to take off her glasses and announce that we might as well get used to being "kissing cousins."

My mother was duly sorry about the pies, but I could see she was gratified that the long interlude spent in walking and waiting outside the pavilion had been spent with a relative. I, for my part, never revealed to her the extent of Betty Jean's interpretation of the expression, "kissing cousins." The incident confirmed a suspicion, however, that education was not confined to school.

Chapter 3

VOCATION?

———◆———

Moods are strange, especially when you're young. At first, I had the sense of being a stranger. This didn't seem possible because I was in familiar surroundings; these were the friends of my childhood and a lot were relatives. But the valley, which once seemed to have the dimensions of a world for roaming, began to close in.

There were tensions. Schoolmates who had failed their high school entrance examinations were becoming rawboned replicas of their fathers. An occasional one who passed seemed relieved when his parents opposed more and higher education.

"I didn't really want to go anyway."

But Billy Jeff said it too often.

"What good is school anyhow?"

Parents often agreed that studying was a feminine trait. We always had female teachers. Yet, going to school didn't benefit girls very much. It was just a ritual. Most parents were anxious to see their daughters marry a man with a minimal mortgage on a farm and book learning might give girls ideas beyond being farmers' wives. And yet there was always the chastening danger of ending up as the unmarried aunt. Practically every valley family had a wraithlike figure of this kind who had somehow missed her chance of becoming a farmer's wife, and whose lack of schooling made her fit for nothing else.

My situation was different, and a ring closed in on me. It wasn't openly discussed. There were simply hints.

"Of course you'll never be satisfied on a farm."

My father said it when I managed while daydreaming to scuffle out several rows of turnips instead of weeds. Then, as if to make amends, I worked like a Trojan in the hay field and collapsed in the heat.

"Don't kill yourself," said Grandfather, "you're not cut out for farming. You read too much. Fellows that read too much never farm well."

At first I thought it was simply my unease and the fact that I had discovered learning. But my mother was aware of the other interests I developed. I found a deep attraction for several girls visiting from the city. It was mutual. Several stopped, while walking, because they said they were thirsty.

"Pretty nice-looking girls," observed Grandfather.

"They're hussies, if you ask me," snapped Mother; "just look at the clothes they wear."

Then, later that night, as if to reassure me, she said, "One thing about it, when you're in a nice boarding school, you won't be having such distractions."

She wouldn't answer any more questions. I sensed overtones of discipline, and there were veiled references to a religious vocation. That was my mother's plan. Father muttered veiled hints about sacrifice.

"It's going to be tough finding the money for everything this fall," he lamented.

"I hope you appreciate what it takes to provide a college education," suggested Mother.

Grandfather signaled me to be quiet. Later he said, "Just remember they want to do the best for you."

"But I don't understand. In a way I want to go—but in another way I don't. Father has one idea, but my mother has something up her sleeve."

He laughed.

"The world is changing, boy, with tractors and motor cars, and telephone even, and the valley is going to change. Farming hasn't been too bad for me and your father—but something else may be better for you. As for your mother, she's got herself thinking you're going to be a priest."

That was a bad enough shock, but the news spread, and I was marked. A visiting lawyer from Handrich stopped me on the streets of Clover.

"I hear you're going to college. Well, you might think of becoming a lawyer, so just remember I'll be glad to have a chat with you any time."

Henderson, the banker, spoke about the promises in banking and invited me to come and see him before I went away. Jimmy Medd, the diminutive tailor, beckoned me into his shop.

"If you're going off to school, lad, you'll want to be as well dressed as possible. Come in and we'll measure you for a suit and it will come mighty reasonable."

I went home confused, with the feeling that I was being pushed. One thing was still to be considered. Where was the money coming from? The depression was becoming more and more apparent, and yet everyone was taking for granted that I would go to college.

Existence at high school with a rented room and communal kitchen had been a mad scramble as assorted students fought off malnutrition with foodstuffs provided by their families over the weekends. Monday and Tuesday were days of plenty, but as the cooked food dwindled and we were left to our own resources, the cuisine became more desperate. By Friday night, we were glad to go home, if only for a decent meal.

Such primitive methods could hardly be introduced to the setting of a college. But Grandfather had an idea. Grandfather had ideas about everything.

"Take your stuff with you and throw it in the pot with the others and you take a share of it. I don't suppose cooking is much different at a place like that than it was for us when we were in the lumber woods."

"Be serious," said Mother, and Grandfather huffed and went over to the neighbors on the Sunday afternoon when the deliberations were going on about my scholastic career. He came back, whistling a tuneless sound. He had either learned something or had been sampling the neighbors' cider.

"You people aren't so smart," he said, prancing into the kitchen, "fussing around here about money for schooling. Well, I got an idea."

"What is it?" demanded Mother.

"One of those scholarships that Tory fellow has been talking about."

The local member of Parliament (a Conservative, much to my grandfather's disgust) had been making speeches about education, saying that he was willing to help boys and girls of the constituency get a higher education.

"Mr. Button?"

Father and Mother said it together and then stopped. The family had inherited deep unfriendliness to Tories. Laurier was still a hero. The conversation raged into the night. Should they approach Mr. Button or not? They were so desperate, Father and I drove to Handrich to see Mr. Button in his apartment at the Royal Exchange.

Mr. Button was our member of Parliament, a very fat man with no neck who rode the dusty side roads and concessions of our county in his Model A Ford coupé looking like an oversize pink bean in a mechanized black pod. Long before I read Mark Twain, I heard Mr. Button say, "There's no trouble in this matter of meeting people and not remembering them or their names. Bless my soul, I do it as easy as can be. When the name doesn't come, I just look at the man and ask him about his old trouble. If it's a woman, I ask her about the old complaint. Every man has a personal trouble and women live by complaints."

In the elegant lobby of the hotel, a lot of people were sitting in easy chairs. It was ten o'clock on a Monday morning and they couldn't be commercial travelers. Father went to the desk where a solemn-faced man with a straggly mustache picked up a telephone with a languid air and spoke into it.

"Just wait over there." He indicated the filled chairs.

We stood awkwardly until a man and his wife got up and followed a girl up the wide stairway. We sat down and I looked at the pictures of faraway places and a pen and ink sketch showing a battle of some kind. The place smelled of varnish, leather, and tobacco smoke. The people in the chairs didn't say very much, but watched as the floor was mopped, the spittoons changed, and the tobacco counter polished by a man with one arm.

The hands of the big clock that was surrounded by advertising cards stood at twelve o'clock before the young lady came and asked us to follow her. I was fascinated by her eyeglasses, which dangled from a black string around her neck.

"Come in. Come in," boomed a voice from the end of the room when we entered the door marked Suite A.

Mr. Button, a mountain of a man, was sitting behind a desk that had clawed feet at each corner. When he put on his glasses, he looked like a cartoon of the man in the moon wearing spectacles.

"My boy, you make me very glad. Want to go on to school. That's the stuff. Too few of our young people realize the golden opportunities that exist for people with an education."

He made little jokes about politics. They were gentle but indicated that he wanted support from the people he helped, even from Grits. He assured me of every support. I was to go to college and there was no doubt about the scholarship. It was simply a matter of details being worked out. He inquired about my mother and my grandfather and the crops. He gave me a handful of pencils with the name of a road contracting firm on them and sent us home elated and somewhat charmed.

The scholarship never materialized. Years later, I met the long-retired Mr. Button and asked him about it. He had shrunk so strikingly that his skin seemed folded over him like an over-size blanket, but he still had the voice.

"My boy," he boomed, selecting a cigar from his pocket and going through the ritual of lighting it. Before my eyes he was performing an illusion, as if re-enacting the role he had played as a member of Parliament.

"My boy, never disappoint people. Never kill their dreams. If I had told you I couldn't pay for the hotel room and had to charge the meals, would you have found a way to go to college?"

We realized right away that Mr. Button was not going to help when father heard in Clover that he was closing his family business. The only thing keeping his creditors at bay was the fact that he was a sitting member of Parliament. The ride home from Clover was a silent affair except for one speech by Father.

"To the best of my knowledge, I have never envied anyone," he said. "Our people came from the potato famine, when our relatives and friends were dying like flies, determined to be eternally grateful for whatever we found. We've done well. At least, none of us has since died from starvation."

He paused then, and didn't answer until we had turned up the side road along the Big Swamp.

"There are times, lad, just like now, when I wish—oh, how I wish, for that extra bit of money that would make it easy to send you off to school."

"I don't have to go to college."

"Oh, yes, you do," he said grimly. "You have to, now."

I didn't understand but I arrived home to something even more ominous. First, Father announced that he had little faith in the member of Parliament.

"What can you expect from a Tory?" demanded Grandfather, somewhat irrationally, since he had suggested it in the first place.

"Father Morrison was here this afternoon," announced Mother.

"I suppose he wants more dues."

"Of course not. He really wanted to see Harry."

My heart lurched.

"See me? What for?"

Grandfather chuckled and I could have cheerfully strangled him on the spot.

"Some girl been complaining."

Mother ignored him in a studied way.

"He may have a way to help Harry get to college."

The more difficult it was for me to go to college, the more determined my mother became. I think Father would have given in, but by this time everyone in the valley was in on the act. I was "the boy who was going to college in the fall."

It took four days for Mother to get me to the brass knocker on the brown-stained door of the rectory. The curtain on the slotlike window was fingered aside and I was eyed by Agatha Phelan. The door opened part way.

"What do you want?"

She sounded as if I had designs on the gold vessels in the church tabernacle. I stammered, but was rescued by the voice of Father Morrison.

"That will be all, Agatha. I asked him to come and see me. In here, Harry."

He was a big man with cigarette ashes graying his black vest, a round, red face, wispy white hair, and pale blue eyes that were as sad as a spaniel's.

"Pay no attention to her," he said, settling in the creaking swivel chair in front of a roll-top desk. "If you ever become a priest, you'll discover that one of the crosses you have to bear is that of having a housekeeper. They all start out humbly and then begin translating between the parishioners and the priest. The next step is when they start acting as translators between the priest and the Creator Himself."

He lit a cigarette and settled back with a whinge of the chair.

"I am delighted to think that one of our boys is entertaining thoughts of entering the priesthood."

This was news to me. I was curious, and so when he finished eulogizing the merits of a vocation, I asked him a question.

"Who is it, Father?"

He roared with laughter.

"The bishop remembers you."

I certainly remembered the bishop. Summoned for some unfathomable reason because of a catechism test I won, I had arrived at the bishop's palace in the nearby town of London. It was late, and the housekeeper gave me supper in a monstrous room where I lay awake all night in a great bed with a canopy. Next morning I desperately wanted to go to the bathroom, and wandering into a room, I chanced upon a man who looked to be seven feet tall pulling on long johns. It was a shock later to find myself serving Mass for the same man, the bishop. I distinguished myself by upsetting the water and wine cruets and ringing the bell for elevation of the Host at the wrong time.

Before I could ask what hell-fire revenge the bishop planned for me, Father Morrison added, "Don't worry. Bishops are human. Even that plant lived."

My face flamed, remembering that I had never found the wash facilities in the episcopal residence.

"Seriously now, do you think your desire to be a priest is firm enough for me to put your case to the bishop. I think he would be willing to help pay your way to college for the two years you need before entering seminary."

The circumstances were closing in like tentacles. There had been stirrings in me from time to time about the priesthood. They came usually in association with reading about faraway missions, the simple grandeur of Benediction, or the overwhelming assault on the senses of midnight Mass. They were familiar to all of us in that time and age, but at that moment they vanished.

"But, Father Morrison, I haven't a vocation."

I said it and waited for an explosion. The pale eyes searched me and they weren't hostile.

"Your mother?"

I nodded.

He nodded.

"Our Catholic mothers are so ardent," he sighed. "Well, I am certainly not going to try and influence you. That's a decision a man must make for himself. It's between you and God. Mothers do try. But don't overlook their determination. There is also an uncanny power in prayer. You are a different boy than most of the lads here. There's an inner drive in you. Your mother sees it as a vocation. It may be. It just may be."

He stood up and put out his hand, saying, "Good luck, and remember my prayers will be with you. Also, I'll be praying for you to make the decision that's best for you. That's important. You must never make a decision of this kind to please someone. It's the matter of your whole life you're dealing with."

All the fuss about college hadn't really bothered me. Even on my way to the rectory, the world seemed shining and bright. When I came out, it was dark. You could compare the feeling to the kind of day when the sun battled clouds in a halfhearted way and the breeze had a chill edge. The leaves would show fluttering, white undersides that helped conjure up strange and uneasy soul feelings. It was, as Grandfather said, like having an itch in your heart you couldn't scratch.

The priest had been kind enough to make me unhappy. If he had attempted to bully, I could have had the satisfaction of being angry. The burningly curious housekeeper watched me from the kitchen window as I went into the church.

St. Peter's was an oasis of quiet peace. I suppose I was actually hoping to find some kind of miracle to satisfy my mother. If it had happened, Father would probably have skeptically accepted it, Grandfather would have been dubious, and Mother would have had another example of the power of prayer.

The Protestants of the community by this time had become reconciled to us. Most of the old-country heritage of bitterness was now saved for the Orange parade on the twelfth of July, and even that was becoming the preserve of a few die-hards.

But the prayer bit was a point of some dissension.

"Do you people really go into church and pray to those statues?"

A girl asked me the question and I was hard put to answer. Yes, we prayed. But the statues just represented saints and we really— and I gave up. My mother, for instance, was constantly in debt to St. Anthony. She kept an open account with him because she was absent-minded and was constantly forgetting where she left stuff.

"Oh, dear St. Anthony, I'll light a candle on Saturday night if you find my glasses."

The glasses would turn up and she would proceed to promise a twenty-five-cent donation to the Mission Box. Then she would lose the tax notice Father had given her for safe keeping, and so it went on. By Saturday night or Sunday, she would have had to employ an accountant to figure it out. Yet, there was in my mind the notion of an almost mystical relationship between St. Anthony and my mother—although as Grandfather said, "If you believe he finds the stuff, you also have to believe he hides it when he's short of prayers or donations."

In our lives from birth to death, the Church was a focal point. People accepted the faith. If they were hard put really to feel the essence of faith, they prayed and went to confession, Mass, and Communion in the solemn belief that faith would be instilled in their hearts in time for that final journey into the unknown. There, they would be rewarded for piety and compensated for the hardships of human existence.

St. Peter's Church smelled of varnish from the pews and the plain, battleship-brown linoleum. There was a muskiness from the stone walls and the lingering odor of incense. The stained glass windows with their angular biblical scenes glowed dully. The guttering, ruby sanctuary lamp spilled color on the garrish face of a crucified Christ. St. Anthony's robes looked dusty. Petals from the vases of peonies had fallen and were splattered on the rug in the sanctuary like splashes of blood.

I went in, sat and waited. When nothing happened I tried the familiar way of pressuring myself. It often was the only way to induce a form of piety before confession. This day it was hopeless.

In spite of all my concentrated thinking about divine shafts of light, inspiration, and revelation, which I had heard the faithful sometimes received, it was apparent I was not one of the chosen.

Then I heard the voice. It clattered into my ears and I looked around to see if Mrs. Wells was in the church.

I was alone!

She was obviously not in church, but when I turned back to the altar, I could hear the rattly voice machine-gunning out the "Holy Mary, Mother of God, etc.," in exactly the same way she did in Lent at the Friday recitation of the Stations of the Cross. She and the priest's housekeeper were often the only ones in attendance, in addition to the separate school students.

I tried to ignore it. It was no use. The voice of Mrs. Wells was a realistic distraction. I fled, conscious of the fact that not only did I not have a vocation, but I was beginning to wonder if I were not losing my mind as well.

It was the longest trip I ever made home in my life. I dallied for as long as possible in the yard before going into the house. The kitchen was pregnant with questions. The table was set for supper and we were having roast chicken. That was a real sign that something was up, because we usually had chicken only on Sundays and during a visit by Father Morrison. I lingered at the washbasin. Grandfather was pretending to be absorbed in the mail-order catalogue. Father was reading the newspaper, using it as a shield so he could neither see nor be seen. Mother was radiantly expectant, eager for good, vocational tidings.

"Come now, folks, and have supper. Harry, I've saved you the liver."

I felt like a condemned man who was being well fed. As I sat down, youthful hunger conquered my reticence. It was a table fit for a king. New boiled potatoes and chicken gravy with flecks of golden crisp. The smell of sage from the dressing was alluring. The golden wax beans were dripping with home-churned butter. Talk swirled around and then stopped. Dead silence.

"Well, did the cat get your tongue? Haven't you any news for us?"

The food lumped in my throat.

"What do you mean?" I muttered.

"Oh, don't keep us in suspense," beamed Mother confidently.

I had to say it. By that time, I couldn't eat anyhow.

"I saw Father Morrison, but I couldn't tell him I wanted to be a priest."

The sounds of that kitchen have haunted me ever since. The clock was ticking, the kettle noisily boiling, and the old dog passed wind in a way that ordinarily would have been funny. No one said anything. We chewed on and finally Mother got up, excused herself, and went into the spare bedroom.

Father cautioned me with a shake of his head to be quiet.

"I can't understand women. If they had their way, the country would be arse-deep in priests," he growled.

It seemed to take an hour for ten minutes or so to go by, and then Mother came back. She checked our plates, poured tea, and sat down. Nothing was said. I had a dreadful desire to please her, but words congealed in my throat. Finally she took an envelope from her pocket.

"I want you to have Mr. Henderson at the bank cash this Victory Bond," she told Father. "Then we'll enroll Harry at St. Gerald's College."

"But that's yours. You had that when we were married," protested Father. "I'll find the money."

"No, I always knew there would be a situation where we absolutely needed this." She said it calmly, but added in a firmer voice: "At that school, under the proper influence, he may well change his mind. At least we'll have the—well . . . I have made up my mind!"

Mother never accepted defeat without a real fight. I was going to college.

Chapter 4

BOOTLEGGER

---◆---

My perspective began to change. There was very little I could do about it, because my family had placed me in a new position. From being an inhabitant of the valley, I had become an observer.

There was my father, for instance. He was a medium-sized man with a balding spot, sun-freckled hands, and sorely tested innate patience. I began to see him as a prisoner, a man who didn't smoke or drink, went to confession on Saturday night, and attended Mass every Sunday without mentioning it.

"A farmer," he said wearily one morning, after an all-night vigil spent waiting for a black heifer to calve, "a farmer waits. He waits and waits and gets damn all for his waiting but a plot in the cemetery."

At another time, it might be a sow with a knack for rolling on or devouring newborn piglets. A horse with an internal infection or chill, after receiving the attention of the veterinary surgeon, would take up nights and sometimes days of attention.

"I don't mind the work," Father would say, "it's the eternal waiting that gets me down. And what for? More of the same."

Mother waited as well. She set eggs to hatch, and watched to make certain a perverse nesting hen did not wander away at a critical time. Dough for baking must rise, cream clot, and butter form in a churn. She planted a garden and guarded it against weeds and pests, knowing that her efforts were indispensable to the livelihood of the farm.

They were patient. I hated the long vigil of holding the reins of the driver or the team while Father stood talking in the bank, food store, or post office. It wasn't helped any by the instructions.

"Now, I've got a chore here, but it isn't worthwhile tying up, so you just wait a minute."

It was years before I realized that my father was pleading for a loan at the bank, soliciting seed, or asking that a due bill at the store be extended. It just seemed that we were not regarded too seriously as far as waiting was concerned; a dentist would leave you with an extended jaw while he talked on the telephone.

Waiting wasn't the only problem. Money was scarce, and I was determined to raise some. The Victory Bond, it was hinted, would pay my tuition. I knew I had to find pocket money. Yet, when I delivered eggs or vegetables to the banker's home or the feed merchant's house, they rubbed it in.

"Why, thank you very much. I don't suppose a boy whose parents can afford to send him to college would accept something?"

When I learned to smile dumbly and (I hoped) pleadingly, they muttered excuses about not having any change.

"I'll catch you next time."

The bane of my existence was the woman who held the mortgage on our place, a large spinster lady in Clover called Miss Hopps. I was constantly having to deliver things such as eggs, pints of cream, and produce to her, and she never once found her purse.

One hot July day, while visiting our place, she shed her corset, a custom-made affair, in our spare bedroom, and went away forgetting it. The following Saturday she telephoned and in a mysterious code explained to Mother that she desperately needed the garment to attend a wedding. Father was going for grist, so I was deputized to take the well-wrapped garment to Miss Hopps.

Several things happened. The wrapping came off the bulky garment somewhat mysteriously on my way uptown in Clover from the grist mill, and I called at Tim Murphy's store, the harness shop, Lee's Café, and Jimmy Medd's Tailor Shop.

When I arrived, the unstayed Miss Hopps, in a flowing garment which made her look somewhat like a perambulating circus tent, grabbed the bedraggled pink corset muttering, "You just wait, you nasty boy! You just wait!"

Kind souls had reported my progress at home, but for some reason my mother was never able to mention it without bursting into laughter. Part of that was because of what happened to the two Hopps sisters in the famous case involving Barney and the hearse.

Barney was the hostler at the livery stable behind the Commercial Hotel. He loved horses and detested automobiles. In spite of the constant reproaches of the Hopps sisters about his drinking in the "back room" of the Commercial, he swallowed his pride and drove them each Sunday to the country in a horse and carriage. He didn't want the livery stable closed by the hotelkeeper, George Warner.

"Cars will be the ruination of the country," maintained Barney, after fortification, because he was usually a timid soul. "They should be outlawed. Their fumes will poison people, and they just gobble up fuel. They're the ugliest creation of man."

We were in the grip of progress, and there was very little Barney could do to prevent it. Men were talking about the new kinds of cars. The sight of a new model or make on Main Street could produce a crowd in no time flat. Then the unkindest cut of all came along. For years, the team of black drivers used on Ab Walker's hearse had been stabled under Barney's care. Ab finally bought a Model T and had a hearse body installed on it. This was, of course, only for summer use, because our spring, winter, and fall roads were generally impassable for cars. But that was small consolation for Barney.

"Imagine the final indignity," he used to say, "of being carted off on your last ride in one of those mechanical boxes, jouncing and banging along with the bad fumes pouring into the faces of the poor mourners."

His complaints were of no avail. Most families plumped for the motorized hearse, when the roads were passable, if only to get a ride in the cars provided for mourners by the undertaker.

"Oh, what a man has to come to," he mourned to my grandfather. "They took Peter Willy McIntyre to his grave today behind the monster. Why, there wasn't a better horseman in the country than Peter Willy, and there he went, choking on fumes, to his last resting place."

It grieved his soul. He naturally gravitated to see Hjalmar Olsen, the blacksmith who drank, and he took Barney to the peace and quiet of the locked smithy. There they ignored the lamentations of Mrs. Olsen and spent the night in a form of wake to the spirit of the man who had loved horses.

Early Sunday churchgoers were startled to hear Barney singing such old lumberjack favorites as "The Jam on Garry's Rock" and "The Maidens of Ontario." These were intermingled with Scandinavian songs, which Hjalmar only remembered under the stimulus of spirits. The concert came to an end when George Warner came to ask Barney if he would take the Hopps sisters for their Sunday drive in the two-seater, horse-drawn carriage.

"Of course," maintained Barney. "I am a man who always puts his duty before pleasure."

There are variations about what happened. Barney said the drivers were in high spirits because they were not getting enough exercise. The Hopps sisters said he drove like a madman and was in no condition to handle horses. Farmers said the team went down the Concession like race horses.

The Hopps sisters, Tilly, the big, corseted one, and Adelaide, thin and sickly, arrived back in a state of nervous exhaustion. Barney put the team away and lack of sleep caught up with him. There was a certain poetic justice in the fact that he found a place to sleep in the hearse, which reposed, when not in use, in the livery stable. After a funeral, Ab carefully took out the crosses from the side windows, if it had been Catholic (or the flower vases, if it had been Protestant), drew the dark blinds on each side, and covered the whole thing with a large tarpaulin.

Ab discovered that, with the symbols removed, he could make a few dollars using it as an ambulance. A methodical man, he installed the stretcher and left the hearse ready for service as a means of transportation for the sick. A number of women, by this time, insisted on having their children in the hospital at Handrich. Since husbands agreed to a hospital delivery with reluctance, it was only natural for them to delay the trip as long as possible, to save on bills for hospital care. Thus, a number of present-day residents of Clover can rightly put down their place of birth as Ab Walker's hearse.

The Hopps sisters, distraught from their trip, decided on late Sunday afternoon to visit Dr. Jamieson for a nerve soother. When they appeared at his office, seeing the hearse standing in front, they paused to speculate. Since the symbols of death had been removed, someone must be having a baby, and pregnancies were news in our community.

Just then, Barney roused himself and opened the blind of the converted hearse to look out. With remarkable presence of mind, he waved. The rest is history.

"Doctor," they screamed, bursting into the office where Jamieson was packing his bag to go on an emergency with Ab Walker in the hastily produced ambulance, "there's a live corpse in the hearse."

The conveyance proved to be empty. Barney by this time had found refuge in the straw mow of the livery stable, where he was discovered, apparently asleep, by the doctor, undertaker, and chattering sisters.

"How long have you been here?" demanded the doctor.

"Why, Doctor," replied Barney, looking confused and rubbing his eyes, "ever since I brought them good ladies home at noon."

They fled, and the hotelkeeper told Barney never to worry

about a job, even if all the horses in the country were replaced by machines.

Incidents such as this were the currency of talk in the valley. At one time they were sufficient to spice the repetitious accounts of trades, deals, and crop reports and keep me interested and amused. Now, they seemed banal; I was plagued by thoughts about going away.

To walk the roads by summer fields and hear the insects humming, cattle digesting their forage, and distant sounds like Kelly's hound baying across the river had once been pleasant. There had been times when skinny dipping by moonlight in the deep hole of the Maitland River or circling the house where the odd Williams brothers lived, making what we thought were unearthly noises, were true adventures.

I couldn't participate any more. It drove the wedge deeper between myself and others of my age. Father Morrison seemed to understand. He employed me for odd jobs such as scything the weeds and burdocks around the cemetery fence and when I didn't want to take money, urged me.

"Take it, lad. When you're at college, you'll need a bit of spare cash. Sweets and things, you know."

Then there was the swamp whisky caper. The Canada Temperance Act was a hard fact in our county. Clergymen and women, with memories of pioneer days when every corner had a saloon dispensing hard liquor at five cents a glass, all welcomed it. Most men observed the formality of openly agreeing with prohibition, while privately flouting it.

Grandfather mourned the passing of the road corner saloons.

"Did people stop at every one?" I once asked him. His forehead wrinkled in concentration.

"No," he laughed, "but I do know your great uncle Mike once set out from Handrich to go to Clover, a distance of nine miles, on a Monday morning and it took him nine days."

The law against liquor was supposed to eliminate it. It didn't work very well. Scattered through a tangled mass of trees, scrub, and marshy ground known as the "Big Swamp," a variety of entrepreneurs distilled a product called swamp whisky. It sold for a dollar a bottle around the fringes of the swamp, or two dollars when peddled at township hall dances.

Swamp whisky quality varied, depending on the distiller. The Jones boys were known to take a great pride in their product and at one time even labeled it. Their still was so well hidden that they were never once raided by snooping constables.

Fly-by-night operators were inclined to pull a batch before it was fully matured. The best description of such a product was given in magistrate's court in Handrich by a man apprehended in a dazed condition by a town constable. The magistrate, known to have a fondness himself for spirits, was curious.

"Charlie," he said, leaning over his desk, "what were you drinking?"

"Swamp," was the reply.

"Where did you get it?"

Charlie looked pained. "Now, Ed—I mean, sir—your majesty —your HONOR—you know I can't tell you."

The magistrate shuffled his papers.

"What did it taste like, Charlie?"

The little man made a face. "Like drinking a mile of barbed wire."

The case was dismissed on a technicality, much to the chagrin of the constable, who worked on a fee system.

In Clover, the Commercial gave a general impression of legality because they sold only pop, tobacco, and cigars in the regular barroom. In the back wall behind the empty bar there was an unpretentious door marked PRIVATE. This led to a short hallway, and a second door opened into the back room. It was plain, with chairs and tables and a small, short counter, presided over by Geroge Warner.

George brought his black, thinning hair forward and kept it plastered down on his skull so that it looked like strands of black, wet yarn. He had little respect for the Canada Temperance Act.

"'Tain't natural," he would say. "Man needs something to relax with. We've had potables since Bible days and them folks that read the Bible misinterpret it."

George was a man of determination. In the back room he had taken the canny precaution of setting his small bar over a well. In the unlikely case of a raid, he would simply dump the stock down the well, which was covered by a set of sliding doors under the bar.

"They'll have to get up early in the morning to get ahead of George," suggested Jake Miller, his friend and hunting companion. George was respected for one thing. He refused to sell whisky under any circumstances on a Sunday and took his baritone voice to praise the Lord at the morning and evening Sunday services of the Presbyterian Church. His Sunday closing was a boon for the other district bootleggers.

An ambitious county constable called Boggs once raided the Commercial. He made the mistake of picking up the Clover town constable, whose wife tipped George Warner by telephone that the raiders were coming. When they broke through the doors dramatically, they found a Saturday afternoon crowd sipping soft drinks.

"Like a cream soda or a root beer?" inquired Warner affably.

Boggs retreated. A new supply had been brought in by the time the Clover constable came back to report that Boggs had returned to Handrich, blazing mad. The crowd settled in to make up for lost time.

"Where's the noise coming from?"

George called for silence. An unearthly sound was coming up from the floor.

"It was like a ghost singing," reported Grandfather, "and then George opened up the doors he had under the bar to cover the well."

"It was Jim Joe Johnston, the odd-job fellow," he said, "recovering. Warner had forgotten about sending him down to fix the cribbing in the well. When George heard about Boggs, he dumped his stock down the well and Jim Joe was about the most surprised man in Clover."

Gramp was a good storyteller. "They hauled Jim Joe Johnston up, although he didn't want to come. They asked him what it was like to have all that booze showering down. Jim Joe was a small man and he was weaving a bit. He just steadied himself on the bar and he said, 'I got clunked on the head and saw stars for a bit and then I shook my head and saw all them bottles floating around and I thought I was dead and in heaven.'"

In a sense this was the background to six o'clock on a Wednesday morning when I was on a wagonload of straw being driven by my cousin Joe Alex to Handrich. We had simply told my parents he wanted me to help him pitch the straw up into the mow of Fegan's Livery Stable and would pay me for it.

Farmers were coming up from doing their chores. Curls of smoke came from kitchen chimneys. It was a beautiful morning—and then Joe Alex explained.

Years later, I saw a movie, *The Wages of Fear*, about desperate men convoying high explosives on a rugged, tropical road, and it brought back the whole episode with sweaty fear. Buried in our load of straw, supposedly going to a livery stable in Handrich, was a cargo of alcohol in five-gallon cans.

It became hot and the horses were inclined to poke at the roadside grass. Joe Alex was nonchalant. I was terrified. The further complication was that everyone we met was inclined to stop and talk. It simply compounded my fears.

"Goin' to Handrich?"

"Yes."

"Gotta load of straw?"

"Yes."

"Didn't know you folks was selling straw?"

"What does Fegan need straw for?"

"Oh—well—those city people from Buffalo have taken to riding horses."

I sweated and Joe Alex dozed. I prodded vainly at the horses.

Finally, at Pepperton, a tiny village near Handrich, an elderly gentleman walking along the road hailed us.

"Would you be kind enough to give me a ride?"

So it came to pass that we arrived in Handrich with a load of straw, a hidden cargo of illegal moonshine, and the Reverend Arthur Janning, a retired minister widely known as "The Booze-hater." I was too young and innocent to realize what a boon he was to the escapade, accompanying us as he did to the livery stable.

"By Godfrey," exclaimed the liveryman, counting Alex out five ten-dollar bills, "if you ever want another job, let me know. That was the slickest trick I ever seen in my life."

The liveryman looked after the unloading, but he was still convulsed when we came back to pick up the team and the wagon with the empty rack. It was an empty moment and not helped when Joe Alex said, "You're leaving in time. It doesn't matter about me, but just wait until people hear you helped take a load of booze into Handrich with old Dry Arthur riding shotgun."

Then he pressed fifteen dollars into my hand.

Chapter 5

AUTHOR

◆

The incident of the straw was never mentioned directly at home, but I was constantly watched. Confession on Saturday nights was mandatory. The older boys romped with frolicking girls down by the lumberyard but I had to be in sight of the family on Main Street. On Sundays, I spent a great deal of time alone—wondering more than daydreaming. My grandfather seemed to understand.

"There's something about you, lad. Like my younger brother. He just lit out one day and never looked back. Fought the Indian wars out in the American West and ended up marrying an Indian woman. Of course, they don't say it in the family, but I often wonder—"

We were on the hillside looking across the place where the creek broke out of the swamp into the pasture field.

"What do you wonder, Gramp?"

"Oh, he wanted me to go too. If I had—well—I guess my life would be a different story. Oh, of course, I don't regret—but—"

His hands rasped as he rubbed them on the knees of his overalls.

"I often speculate, as you might say, on what might have been. Stayed here all my life and never did see much or do much—"

I felt the chasm that opened up in him letting a cold breath out. He stopped it by putting his hand in his pocket and handing me a wadded up ten-dollar bill.

"Maybe you don't need this, but take it. You may be able to pick up a few straw jobs around school."

He put the accent on straw, grinned and stood up, and we walked back to the house. In my room there was the old, tin trunk which had been given a coat of black enamel. It could have been a coffin for a midget.

That night I wakened in the hot darkness. The valley was breathless. On the chair there was the tweed suit, my new armor, bought by my parents, who equated thickness with serviceability. The next memory is of sweltering in the suit on the station platform at Clover. Getting ready for the train, Ben Black, the station agent, creaked on his wooden leg. Two men sat on cream cans in the shade. Cattle bawled in the stock pens waiting for Tuesday shipment to Toronto.

"Sure is hot."

Father stared past the water tower as if there was something of deep fascination in the distance.

"Sure is. 'Minds me of the time we went West on the harvest excursion and it was doggone hot then too. Sweat buckets."

Mother was fussing about the things she had packed for me.

"Your socks are on the left-hand side in the trunk. Oh, dear, did I remember to put in those handkerchiefs after I ironed them?"

"Yes, Mother. I saw you put them in."

Then an awkward silence developed. Grandfather, with his reminiscences pushed to the limit, went back to fiddling with his pipe. Father saw Mr. Black start to wheel the express truck out, and this gave him the excuse to check the time by the station house clock. We watched the pantomime until he came back.

"Be here in eleven minutes."

Eleven minutes seemed a very long time. Ben McGrath, the section foreman, wheeling the little handcar off on the siding, paused a moment to mop his red, flushed face.

"By golly, lad, you better be careful when you get to the city. I knew a man once went to that same place and he got lost and was never heard of again."

Mr. Black, having arranged express and freight for the train, came over.

"I'll tell the conductor to be sure and warn you in plenty of time before you get to the junction where you have to change."

Dire premonitions clutched my heart. It was my first train trip, let alone changing from one train to another.

"My trunk?" I blurted.

Ben Black twinkled.

"Nothing to worry about. I'm having that checked through for you. Just go to the baggage office when you get to the city and show them the stub with your ticket."

That set off a search for the ticket, and the fuss used up some of the waiting minutes. Grandfather slapped me on the shoulder and told me to behave. Father gave me some extra change and Mother stood there with a handkerchief poised for tears.

"Good-by," I croaked in the voice of the condemned, and stumbled up the steps.

The conductor nudged me over to the other side of the train where I could watch my family, somehow now seemingly driven into a tight group. After what seemed like hours, the train finally pulled out.

Then I began to notice the other people on the train. The thought of sharpies and gamblers made me feel the wet wad of money pinned to my underwear. I checked the ticket again, counted and recounted the change in my pocket, and resisted the temptation to buy a magazine.

The valley was slipping by the windows. There was the Myers bush where we went to sugaring-off parties. Joe Findley was stalled by the township road and had the hood up on his gray Dort. Fields, trees, houses, and even the clouds were vanishing. I was losing my world, and when we crossed the river bridge and I saw the naked boys making plunges into the water, I was sadder than I had ever been before in my life.

It was as if I would never see this place or my family again. But then, I discovered an extra bundle. My mother had pushed it into my hands as I was leaving. Checking to make sure the wad of bills was still pinned to my underwear, I opened the parcel. By the time I had eaten the second chicken sandwich and the conductor had punched my ticket, the sadness began to leave. I kept my coat on in spite of the heat because I was afraid of losing it.

I suppose I would have liked the trip to go on for a much longer time, but the change of trains was accomplished smoothly and we arrived at New Gordon only thirty-five minutes behind schedule.

"You going to St. Gerald's?"

The stooped man with the battered cap and the blue denim apron brought me back to the reality of the New Gordon station platform.

"Y . . . yes . . . sir."

I had managed the trip from our country station to Clover, through the intricacy of a station change and arrived safely at the college city.

"What's your name?"

I don't know what would have happened if my name had not been on the sheaf of flimsies he took from his hip pocket. He was brusque in the manner of people who have no real authority and have a bristling attitude of defense.

"Gimme your baggage check and I'll take your trunk up to the school."

I fussed like a panicky caterpillar in my cocoon of oversize and overthick tweed to find the tickets. Something about my nervousness must have softened him a bit because as he took the check he said, "Leave your valise and I'll take that along. Too heavy to lug by yourself."

"But . . . but . . . what . . . I mean . . ."

"Nothing to worry about, son, or don't you know where the place is?"

I didn't. I didn't even know my way around the city.

"Take that street up there and keep on going across Main

Street," he said, pointing with his pipe. "Lots of other young fellows going that way. You can't miss the place."

I wanted to be sure.

"What does it look like, sir?"

It may have been my fear. It may have been calling him "sir." He stopped, slipped his cap back on his head, raked his hair with his fingers, and grinned.

"Big and ugly. Red brick. Something like a jail."

Even in the station I was surrounded by noise and the sounds of reunion. I felt as if I were the only stranger. The others wore an astonishing variety of clothes, and the occasional boy stared at me in an almost rude way, as if to determine if it were possible that a human being would inhabit such clothing on a hot September day.

The old porter was called "Jimmy," and it was apparent he remembered some of the students with pleasure and some with less than favor.

"You back?" he said to a big and loud blond lad with wisps of unshaven fuzz on his face like tufts. "I thought you flunked out last year."

"Haw . . . haw . . . haw . . . fooled you, Jimmy," the lad said, tipping the old gentleman's cap forward on his forehead, "my old man gave them a big donation."

Even a small city like New Gordon appeared to be an impossibly large metropolis to a boy from an isolated Western Ontario valley. Cars and trucks at home were still almost a novelty. Here scores of them went whizzing by with abandon, and the mystery was the power of the traffic lights. Everybody obeyed the lights, but I was afraid they would suddenly go wild while I was in the middle of the street. All kinds of visions of disaster flashed in my mind. After a time, I became aware of a small boy with thick glasses who was obviously stalled like myself.

"They switch pretty fast," he said sheepishly.

I agreed, but his helplessness fanned some slight feeling of leadership in me as I said, "Come on, let's go."

We made it as triumphantly as Columbus on arriving in America.

"My name is Otto," he said, "and if you don't mind, I'll walk with you because I don't see distances too well."

Having somebody depend on me worked wonders. We had to get to the school. It didn't work out very well. I took a wrong turning, and we came to an area where there was no sign of students. Otto didn't complain, except to say once that he understood the college was only three blocks from Main Street. Then the old truck driven by Jimmy wheezed by and he waved me in another direction.

"It's not really this far," I said. "I thought a walk after the train trip wouldn't be a bad idea."

St. Gerald's was a mass of red brick that looked unplanned. In today's jargon, it would be a happening. No two of the adjoining buildings were of the same height. The whole place was surrounded, except for the forbidding entrance way, by the kind of high fence customarily seen around a jail. When I looked down the driveway past the main building, there was a profusion of cindered grounds and a small oasis of green surrounding a statue. I later found out it was that of a prosperous plumber by the name of Gerald who left part of his fortune to the school. The greenery was protected by a chain-link fence, and this was where the teachers took protected walks. The whole place had a penal atmosphere, infected by the smell of cooking which Otto suggested was like "moldy washing."

Registration was my first experience in total bedlam. One moment they seemed to be registering alphabetically. The next minute, you were shunted into a priority line, only to discover that this was for second-year students. You could also be pushed out the front door altogether and find yourself at the end of the line.

Otto (whose last name was Alberts) and I were finally registered and sent to the dormitory. This enclosure was on the top floor of the seediest-looking building of the lot. There were two

bull pens with cots jammed all over them and a furious fight going on for space. Veterans wanted cots beside the windows. Older
boys pre-empted cots by the fire exits and stairs. We merely
wanted cots, and were put against the partition between the senior and junior dormitories. We had lockers in the washrooms and
the prefect was a tired-eyed individual who appeared to approve
of the fact that I was from the country.

"Just don't take any bilge from anybody," he advised me, "don't
let them push you around. Most of these town lads are pests and
spoiled. Only reason they're here is because they've been kicked
out of better schools. This place will take anybody. It's a bloody
reform school for rich kids and a refuge for poor ones."

We survived supper. It was an experience. Several of the priests
ranged around like herdsmen to get order in the place, but we ate
something, and then wandered about the cinder-strewn campus.

"Hey you!"

The big, blond boy with the tufted face was yelling at me. I
didn't answer. He persisted, "Where you from?"

Then I made the fatal mistake of saying, "Clover," and he ex-
ploded, calling everyone to come and see "the hayseed from
Clover."

Otto drew himself up to his four-feet-eleven and said, "Oh, shut
up, you bully," and the big boy guffawed. "Look, the hayseed's got
a seeing-eye mouse. Red and his seeing-eye mouse."

That's how nicknames were born. They persisted to the point
where even the teachers used them. But I didn't know, and so I
lashed out at the taunter.

I was younger, but work in hay and grain fields had toughened
me to the point where strength and, more probably, surprise, carried the bully to the cinders. I was busy bloodying his nose when
a black-clad disciplinarian lifted me away. I think he smiled when
someone explained the cause of the fight, but I went to bed that
night certain that I was going to be expelled.

Later in the night, when the dormitory had settled down, I

heard a whisper from Otto, who said, "Gosh, Red, I want to thank you. Nobody ever stuck up for me before."

The two dormitories were on the top floor of what was called the "Recreation Building" at St. Gerald's College. The basement, first, and second floors had an auditorium, a swimming pool, which leaked too much to be used, a gymnasium, and a nest of smaller rooms. These were constantly being opened and relocked by mysterious lay workers of the college, all of whom seemed to have taken perpetual vows of silence so far as the students were concerned.

The dormitory floor had private rooms for the junior and senior prefects, a large locker room and washroom, and the two dormitories. The senior, L-shaped one was called the "Bull Pen" and the smaller one, nestled in the lee of the L, was for juniors and therefore became the "Monkey Ward." The windows on the street side were covered by wire mesh to try to prevent the students from annoying passing girls. They still tried to attract attention through the screen, giving many residents of New Gordon the impression that the building was a place of confinement for the insane. Thus, the dormitory building was called the "Nut House" by students. Clerical teachers objected. The lay teachers seemed amused.

The evening study period was over at nine o'clock. At nine-twenty the dormitory lights flashed a warning. At nine-thirty the lights went out and if you were still dawdling in the washroom, it meant you had to chart the dangerous corridors between the rows of cots. There were many obstacles.

"Who's that?" You were challenged.

"It's Red."

"Snap it up."

If you were safe, you could scurry on to your own bed. If you were in bad with the ruling clique, you had to brave the torture route, starting with the frame-up. There would be the swushing sound of bare feet, whispers, and commotion, followed by the unearthly sounds of someone being dumped from bed. Figures streaked by you and cots creaked, and then the light came on and a scowling senior prefect was staring at you. There you stood, like a fox in a chicken yard covered with feathers.

"What have you got to say for yourself?"

The prefect knew you were innocent. The boy dumped on the floor in a cascade of sheets and blankets knew you were blameless. Everyone knew you had been framed, but there was the evidence. Sometimes the prefect tried to square it by sending you off to your own cot and making four of the older strong-arm boys clear up the mess. That wasn't very good either, because it simply meant that they found an even more exquisite form of torture, such as giving you a French sheet.

Everyone delayed getting into bed till the last moment. You would even stand beside your cot watching the hand of the prefect moving toward the light switch as he read his watch. Just as he touched the switch, you grabbed the covers and jumped into bed.

"ZUNK-K-K!"

If your feet came solidly into contact with the top sheet folded back and your toes numbed, you were a French sheet victim. The normal thing would have been to check the sheets before getting into bed, but that was strictly taboo. Just as members of the French Foreign Legion or penitentiary inmates had codes of behavior, so also did the residents of the "Bull Pen."

If you sneaked a look and were seen, an even more horrible surprise could be prepared. You simply cannot imagine the scratching torment of trying to sleep in a bed which has been doused with finely chopped horsehair. Similarly, I have witnessed a fellow inmate leaping in the air and howling like a wounded banshee when his feet came in contact with a piece of liver or a dead fish.

By night, with only a faint light coming in from outside, the dormitory was a place of mystery. Creeping figures might snake under your bed on their way to the "Monkey Ward" to blackmail treats from juniors with affluent parents and liberal allowances.

I soon learned that some of the older students used the stairs of the fire escape to make romantic forays into the city.

On moonlit nights there was the atmosphere of a pantomime. Being a freshman, you kept your head down and your mouth shut. It was especially dangerous at the full of the moon because prankish notions invaded the minds of even the most staid seniors.

Noise was the most difficult thing to get used to. There was never a time of silence. The building creaked and groaned as if the structure was tired and complaining of age. In windy weather it seemed like a ghostly galleon breaking up on the rocks. Cot springs creaked, the sleepers turned and were restless, and we had every known variety of snorer in recorded history. From high-pitched, tremulous squeaks to deep, sawing barrel tones, there was never a time during the night when the dormitory didn't sound like a marsh full of neurotic frogs.

I lay awake that first night, and tried to remember my room at home where the only loudness was the soft, soothing sound of the pine boughs at the window. Was education really worth this effort? Yet, there had been an imperceptible change in my attitude. I realized now that it had been going on for much longer than I had known. I had been touched by something which drew me away from the valley. I wondered about the tepid spring day when a teacher of English literature had penetrated my daydreaming. He was a frustrated poet who had made me feel the power of poetry.

While working in my uncle's store, I had written an essay eulogizing the overalls made by the company sponsoring the essay contest. The overalls, identified by a railroad car and a heart, were absolutely essential in my imaginary life as a transcontinental railroad engineer. To the chagrin of my entire family, I received a prize of six pairs of overalls, size forty-six, and a letter from the president of the company inviting me to stop over for lunch whenever my transcontinental duties allowed it.

I never managed the lunch. My uncle was furious, expecting at any time to have police officers raid our place just to prove my flagrant dishonesty. Budding genius had been nipped—but on that spring afternoon in school it was reawakened.

Mr. Cartwright, the poetic professor, had a form of inspiration in his plea for the creative life of man. With a few words he dismissed the passing phenomena of financiers, politicians, and career men. They were merely selfish players on the stage of life. The men and women who would contribute to the heritage of life were the creative ones. Wealth, pomp, and glory would pass and crumble but the inspired world of literature and art was the only legacy man would have in generations to follow. When "Carty" was talking, Plato, Shakespeare, Dickens, Wordsworth, Galsworthy, Chesterton . . . were alive and in the classroom.

The trance of his presence was lost on most of the students, but it lingered with me. I went to the rooming house to contemplate my future. Up to this time, thoughts of a career had been entwined with a desire to find a job that had the least work and the most money attached. Now, with the fervor induced by the teacher's words, I decided to become a writer.

I had to start writing immediately. I had a scribbler and two pencils. My jam-eating roommate was asleep. I must write a story. After about five pages and a hundred false starts, it was evident that I didn't have any inspiration. Coupled with that was the annoying snoring of my companion. I retired to an old bench in the back yard.

"What are ya doin'?"

This was my first audience. She was a small child in a dirty dress who seemed, for the moment, to be impressed by my answer.

"Writing."

To dramatize my effort, I idly scribbled words on the paper. "You writin' a letter? Ma wrote about the relief."

This was sheer inspiration. Relief! Hard times were all around me. Cartwright had stressed the importance of writing about what a person knew from his own experience and understanding. I started:

"*The cold, hard face and the mean, squinting eyes of the relief officer peered at the poor, unfortunate man.*"

The waif lost interest and departed, but not before shattering my warm feelings of companionship with the underprivileged.

"Relief man said he wouldn't give another cent if my old man didn't stop boozing."

I didn't know how to cope. I didn't know anything about relief. I would have to do some research if the story was going to be valid. I remembered that the township clerk was responsible for relief and so I went to the town hall.

The township offices and the town hall offices were closed. There wasn't even a vagrant in the lockup. Since research was barred, it seemed reasonable to go to the poolroom. I lost twenty cents at blackjack.

My family was puzzled that weekend. My mother wanted to give me sulphur and molasses. My father yelled at me for dropping potatoes in the furrow in a haphazard manner. Grandfather was curious.

"Are you in any trouble?"

"Oh, I'm feeling fine, Gramp, I've come to a big decision. A really important decision."

He puffed on his pipe, still obviously puzzled.

"Behind in your lessons?"

"No, but I'm going to be a writer."

He puffed for some time. "A writer. That's all right. What are you going to do for a living?"

I didn't realize, in my own fervor of the moment, just how much wisdom there was in his words. It took many years to comprehend their significance.

Sleep was a wonderful relief when it finally came in the noisy dormitory.

Chapter 6

FOOD

◆

We were herded into a damp subterranean auditorium, directly under the leaky swimming pool and gymnasium. A nervous priest walked across the stage, absent-mindedly reading his office. Finally an assembly of priests swept him into the wings, taking chairs at the back of the stage. There were two lay teachers. One looked like a defrocked, fat monk with a tonsure of hair around his bald head. The other was a thin, nervous character who kept reaming his ear and examining his pinkie for evidence of wax.

The rector swept in, nodded to the staff, and stood solidly on his two feet at front stage. He smoothed his soutane over the bulge of his stomach, shoved his hands into mysterious pockets, and cleared his throat.

"The purpose of your stay at St. Gerald's College is to acquire an education and training which will fit you for the struggle in life out there."

He flung his black arm in an impressive gesture indicating the world outside our enclosed scholastic world. We were, it would seem, safe and sound inside the barricades.

"We are here to help you."

A backhanded gesture indicated the group of soutaned teachers and the two bewildered civilians.

"We are guides and friends on your adventure in learning. Of course, if you are to make the best of this experience, there are a few simple rules which must be adhered to."

He smiled, and after pausing to make certain of our absorption of the rationed warmth, proceeded to bend and tie us with the "do nots." They were impressive and frightening and, as we discovered later, irksome.

Girls were taboo. They were, in simple fact, anathema.

"Nothing can be as destructive in your adolescence as the fancy of romantic attachments. They will destroy your reason and power to concentrate. We shall take a most serious view of any adolescent trifling which endangers your moral and scholastic future."

There was a long, painful pause. Then, he went on to thunder out rules about punctuality, neatness, and deportment. During the infrequent times we were to be allowed downtown in the wicked city, we must be especially careful. We were representatives of St. Gerald's. We must act at all times as ambassadors of the college and uphold the tradition of gentlemen of scholarly and serious moral intent. We were to be living examples of decorum, chastity, and honesty.

We who came from country and isolated places were impressed and awed. In fact, we were terrified.

"Aw, he's a windbag," declared an American boy called Johnny King. "I heard that baloney last year. When *he* went to school here, they say he was a real heller. . . . Just remember, it's them or us!" To anyone raised with the deferential attitudes to priests of the country, this approached heresy, or what we dimly thought heresy must be.

In the country, clergymen, Catholic or Protestant, were unreal. Custom placed them on pedestals. When the priest came to call, Mother ushered him into the front parlor, Father made a race to change his clothes, and we sat around and talked in stilted phrases. A minister in Handrich who played golf was a minor sensation for a time. When our priest bought a blue car in place of a black one, some of the congregation thought he was losing his faith.

Now, at college, clergymen lived near us, supervised us, taught us, ate only slightly better food in the same dining room, and played games with us. I can still remember the shock of seeing a husky young priest lift the skirts of his soutane and kick a football with his tremendous boots.

Bit by bit, we discovered their natural qualities. These were not supernatural. They had been lads like ourselves who came to the college, many as green as the hills of their home farms, and somehow lived through the armylike discipline and stayed on to be ordained to become teachers.

But there were barriers between students and priests.

"Now, you lads," rasped Father Greggs, the disciplinarian, a giant of a man with hamlike hands, "I just want to warn you. I know all the tricks. Don't forget I went through here and I tried every trick you can think of, and maybe more. So don't try them on me."

But there were ways to avoid a boring constant regimen. A slight sore throat, aided by a few vigorous turns around the gym track and a hot shower, could give you an excused day in bed, without having to go to the infirmary. A woebegone look and reddened eyes worked with one teacher, if you played it so that he asked you what the matter was. You told him, "a headache," and he excused you because he himself suffered from migraine. A nervous one could be discomposed into forgetting assignments by a careful mixture of the casual noises of desks squeaking, boots scraping, pencil sharpening, and chalk rasping.

They were human beings. They too had moods. Some were scrupulously fair and others played favorites. Some were vain and others were so humble they made us feel dishonest. Some were so quick-tempered that they made bad judgments. Even timid wee Otto, detained for punishment, became an enemy of one teacher, although he had determined to be co-operative.

"I told him I didn't do it," he said tearfully. "I wasn't lying. I told him and he wouldn't believe me. You know, Harry, around this place, it's really them or us. We can't let them win."

The teachers at St. Gerald's College appeared to pride themselves on the ruggedness of the system. They made references to the virtues of strict discipline and the absence of softening body comforts. We were constantly being served apt quotations about the Spartans.

> *Earth, render back from out thy breast*
> *A remnant of our Spartan dead!*
> *Of the three hundred grant but three,*
> *To make a new Thermopylae!*

We were shy of heat in the classroom that day and Otto, my diminutive friend, shivering said:

"There may only be three of us left by spring if they keep this up."

When our teeth did chattering dances the next morning because the pipes had burst, I was ready to believe him. The general impression was that the buildings were kept at a sufficiently chilly state to keep all the students awake. It had other effects.

"Please, I can't do this work."

"Why not, may I ask?"

"My hands are too cold."

Whack! Whack! The ruler snapped on the chilled hands of the protesting boy.

"You see, lad, they're certainly not too numb to miss feeling that."

Another had a cynical way of saying, "Now, my good little Spartans, rub your hands together briskly and you'll feel a whole lot better. This is a training for real men."

Then he would proceed vigorously to thump circulation into his own hands while the pupils sheepishly tried the same thing.

The heating situation set off a general round of complaining.

"It would serve them right if a whole bunch of us took sick and died. You watch and see if there aren't some pneumonia cases. Damn wonder somebody hasn't come down with it already."

The senior boy said it with such vehemence that he appeared to want a volunteer. None of us were ready for such drastic measures, however, and the matter was dropped. Then a dramatic thing happened. At dinner, just before the final grace, the senior stood up and read a petition to the faculty. It was lengthy and couched in a schoolboy's idea of legal phraseology. When the petitioner took his seat, we expected that he would be given a real dressing down. Instead, the disciplinarian responded politely, almost too politely.

"I appreciate your frankness, and we shall take the matter under consideration."

The whole affair shocked us. Bill, who made the plea, was like a victorious gladiator for a time. He discovered he had won a hollow victory. The radiators bounced with heat. The dormitory was stifling. Teachers and prefects resisted our pleas to open the windows, and one night in particular, when the weather turned mild, we lay on our cots gasping like beached fish. Then the Spartan system was reinstated. I suppose the staff were also suffering from the unusual heat.

St. Gerald's was a low-cost institution in a small Ontario city at a time of depression. It had a reputation for discipline. As a result, it attracted a mixed group of students. They eyed one another with suspicion during the first days on the cindered and asphalt-covered campus which separated the buildings from the somewhat limited area devoted to courts for tennis and handball and the playing field. We hadn't heard of concentration camps in those carefree days, but we were affected by the physical layout of the place.

In the first few days returning students renewed acquaintance-ships and gossiped without paying attention to us. Newcomers moved around reluctantly and timidly, hoping that tentative bits of conversation might flourish into friendships to combat the loneliness.

"You new here?"

He was a fierce-looking little boy with a face that was old for his body. We heard vaguely that his family had money and he had been expelled from several schools.

"Yes," I said.

"Old enough to smoke?"

"No. Not legally, anyhow."

"How come you're so big, then?"

That was a stumper so I avoided an answer.

"What difference does it make?"

"Well, I'll pay you a dollar a week to carry my smokes. They won't bother you for smoking."

Freddy was addicted to smoking, and his parents had left instructions that he was to be kept from it. Two days at school and he had already paid one of the engineers for the privilege of smoking in the boiler room. He had also contracted with a student librarian for use of the storeroom behind the library and now he was looking for a cover in the open space. "All you have to do is grab the cigarette if one of the black widows comes near, and carry the smokes." To him all teachers who wore black cassocks were "black widows." He appeared to have unlimited spending money.

My clash and sheer luck in downing the bully had left Otto Alberts almost as a charge.

"I have to go to school," he said despondently, at one recess time.

"Why?"

"Because I'm too small to do anything else. I got sent here because my dad is six-feet-two and thinks I'm a freak."

Peter King, on the other hand, was a giant, with a sense of humor.

"Look at those," he said, displaying his custom-made, size fifteen shoes. "And remember that my mother's hobby is collecting miniatures."

Peter played rugby for St. Gerald's until one wet day when the field was muddy and soggy. The opposing team was a light one and

Peter claimed that he was benched because he accidentally stepped on an opposition lineman and squashed him into the field.

"Boy, is this a dump! My old man must be going rockers to send me to a place like this. It won't take long to get bounced out of here."

Willy Buler paced the inside of the red board fence and lamented his lot. American-born, he had been dismissed from four native and three European schools. He also managed, by his attitude, to bring the sense of nationalism of every Canadian to a full boiling point. I don't suppose that in the history of St. Gerald's College there was ever a fuller and more biased account of the War of 1812 given than that year's.

Country boys were attracted to each other. Hardships didn't bother us as much as city-bred youngsters. We marveled at the affluent South American students and rearranged our thoughts about a continent that we had assumed was backward. There were shy boys, bad boys, innocent boys, greedy boys, and some very sharp characters at the college.

Lennie was pencil-thin and sharp-featured. Mel was squat with a somewhat hairy face. They were inseparable and always seemed to be in conversation with one other student. They spent all their spare time in these whispered sessions, which appeared conspiratorial.

Finally it was my turn and I learned what they were all about.

"You smoke?" asked Lennie, offering me a slender, hand-rolled cigarette.

"No. Well, in a way. I have a deal if I want to."

"Oh," said Mel, taking the cigarette from Lennie's hand and replacing it in a tin box, "if you ever need cigarettes we sell them six for five cents."

"We also lend you money," supplied Lennie, "twenty cents during the week and you pay us twenty-five on Saturday."

Our society was complete. St. Gerald's College had its confidence men.

Saturday was a magical day for students whose parents had

deposited spending money for them with the bursar. It was allowance day as well for wealthy South American students, whose private caches of money had been expropriated by the school authorities in an attempt to maintain some democratic uniformity. The wealthy students, however, did have extensive wardrobes. Tony, from Argentina, had six trunks and when he was refused money by the bursar he held a rummage sale. Tony accepted almost any bid, replenishing his wardrobe by simply writing the family lawyer in New York for replacements, which were sent without delay. This formed the basis of a flourishing black market.

A sweater which you bought for fifty cents in warm weather when Tony was desperate to buy chocolates or go to a show on a free afternoon, might be resold for two or even three dollars in cold weather. I later discovered that Tony's clothes were British-made, and the sweater had cost perhaps twenty dollars. Country boys couldn't imagine a sweater being worth that much. Our suits cost less.

Two enterprising characters took orders for toothpaste, shaving cream, and other staples and delivered such small commodities for anything between ten and twenty cents.

"Where are you fellows getting this stuff?" demanded Peter King, after buying a toothbrush and shaving cream for twenty-five cents.

"Oh," said the blinky boy, pointing to his partner, who served as lookout at their favorite trading spot behind a monument on the campus, "his uncle buys up stuff at fire sales and we get it there." This explanation dissolved when they were caught sneaking in through an arrangement of loose boards in the high fence. They had been downtown without official leave. The reverend disciplinarian was suspicious of the fullness of their bulky plus fours. The reason became apparent with the arrival of a policeman and the manager of a local five-and-ten-cent store. They vanished from St. Gerald's. We were given a lecture in the assembly hall about being accessories to crime.

We craved sweets as a change to the monotony of our diet. A

boy who received a parcel from home had as great an advantage as the recipient of a prisoner-of-war package. He could get homework finished, have his bed made, or make a swap for a tie or a pair of socks for sweets of any kind. The making of a bed was important because prefects exercised army-camp discipline, and woe betide the unlucky bad bedmaker. Some boys could never manage a neat bed and so communal life was helped by the barter system.

We were always thinking about food. It ranked with sex. Otto Alberts and I attached ourselves to Johnny King, Bill Singer, a melancholy lad called Titus Maloney, and a madcap, Tommy Whelan. We scrounged a table in the dining hall for ourselves and the disciplinarian installed the Mills twins with us. They were lookalikes from Saginaw in Michigan; a teacher threatened to have them tattooed One and Two.

The dining hall was an enormous bare room with tables set for eight. The staff sat at a long table on a platform and faced the room. At the other end the serving apertures (called the "troughs") opened from the kitchen. There was a pulpitlike affair in one corner of the room where the disciplinarian made announcements, the rector gave sacred readings at retreat time, or where an unruly boy was sent to say the rosary aloud at mealtime as punishment. The tables were covered with white oilcloth. The dishes and cutlery were stacked in the center of each table. As soon as grace was spoken there was a general grab for the implements of eating. It was hotly contested, since there was usually a shortage of something. If you ended up without a plate or a spoon or a cup, the chances of getting one were slim. The boys who waited on tables to help make up tuition performed a minimum of work in as surly a way as possible.

The kitchen was presided over by a silent brother with a shaved bullet head and equally taciturn workers. It was a gloomy place of black stoves, large containers, and constant clouds of steam. It smelled like a laundry.

For our first breakfast, we had milk, oatmeal porridge with

plenty of husks, brown sugar, bread and butter and jam, very weak coffee and wieners.

"Boy, are we having a treat," exclaimed Johnny, a veteran. "Wieners! And it isn't a Thursday. Every Thursday, we get three wieners apiece. Not two wieners. Not four wieners. You have a constitutional right to three. Now, let me tell you—the waiters will try to steal them. Other students will try to cheat you. But, remember, you must stand up and demand your share. Three wieners." He further mystified us by wrapping one of his weiners in a piece of paper and putting it in his pocket.

"That's for trading," he said.

Wieners were the only break in monotonous breakfasts. We had shriveled bacon one morning, and eggs cooked into a gooey mass the next. The bread was puttylike. The jam, according to boys with experience, was concocted in the kitchen from turnips and timothy seed with artificial color and vague sweetenings.

The wieners were a treat, and we were even allowed mustard. We ate mustard sandwiches on the mornings when the barter system had appropriated the wieners. I could never tell my mother about any of it. Punishment and a Spartan discipline she would be able to understand, but never starvation.

The place also abounded in myths. Older students said the oatmeal was purchased in open truckloads and dumped each fall in vast underground bins. One of the silent employees kept busy killing mice and rats down there, so you had to be careful in eating it that you didn't come on mouse droppings, or more. Rats were kept for the stew! That's what they said—and we more than half believed it.

The stew was celebrated. I once saw the Mills twins turn green and faint, in unison, when Johnny King pulled a strip of something from between his teeth, saying, "Rat fur. Can't these bloody people learn how to skin rats?"

Fridays were a horror. They purchased fish from some remote source, and New Gordon was an inland city where refrigeration was still primitive. Once, when the weather turned warm, the rankness of our dinner became evident all over college by mid-afternoon. The dining room smelled like the hold of an ancient fishing trawler. The fish was disguised in a sticky cream sauce. We tried to eat it and almost choked. The staff looked flustered. The rector smiled blandly and dug in. He chewed with every eye in the room on him. Then he gagged and brought the napkin up to cover his face. The fish was recalled, and we were given tinned salmon from a stock kept for visits by the bishop or prominent parents.

I longed for the madness of Miss Emily's rooming house. We talked constantly about food, and in the middle of the night you heard the evidence of trading. A boy in plain hunger would start canvasing.

"You got anything to eat?"

"Some chocolate."

"Give you . . ."

With the deal made, the seller would creep out to the locker room. A deal could usually be arranged with Alex, who kept a stock of hard summer sausage, brought from his father's country butcher shop. The trouble with Alex was high, high prices.

Many a student, neatly making Alex's bed or shining his shoes two weeks after satisfying one nocturnal hunger, tried to conjure up memories of the salami feast as compensation.

Chapter 7

INITIATION

———◆———

Initiation at St. Gerald's was a barbaric rite. The threats began as soon as you arrived.

"Initiation is really going to be something this year."

"Yeah, Tom Begley was hurt last year and he sure is going to make up for it this year."

First-year students lived in fear and apprehension. At the first breakfast, Peter, the hulking hero of St. Gerald's rugby team, looked up with his mouth full of food and spluttered:

"I'm going to be in charge of the electric chair at the initiation. We're going to use the full limit of juice this year. Just short of death. We were too gentle last year. Only three went to the infirmary."

Otto Alberts abruptly lost his appetite.

"D-d-did you hear what he said about the—the electric chair?"

"Oh, he's just a blowhard," I said, trying to muster a very frail courage.

It was difficult, however, because the whole yard was dotted with self-conscious groups of freshmen trying to mask their fears. Then the fifth columnists started.

"You fellas new here?"

We were willing, out of fear and loneliness, to make friends with anyone. We would respond and they would take up their role.

"Things aren't so bad here. Not bad at all. You're not scared of initiation are you?"

"Oh, no, we know it's just play-acting."

The false friend would nod.

"That's right. Just don't panic. I went through it last year and there was nothing to be afraid of, but mind you, one word of warning. If you've got a weak heart or anything, be sure and tell one of the teachers—especially the disciplinarian. They don't want a repeat of what happened last year. That was awful. Gosh, I'll never forget it."

That set everybody off. Some developed maladies, throwing themselves on the mercy of the doctor and the nurses at the infirmary. After receiving a succession of none too gentle purgatives, they were forced to admit defeat. At that point the gullible ones tried to cultivate sympathy on the part of the disciplinarian. He was a lean, athletic man whose main characteristics were a booming laugh and an attitude of perpetual motion. His voice carried through walls and down corridors.

"Got a bad heart, eh? Well, my boy, I suggest you get a doctor's certificate. We'll excuse you then. Can't do it without a certificate. Wouldn't think of doing it anyhow. Think initiation is good for any boy. Toughens them up. Makes men of them. Now, move along, boy. Don't loiter. You must have something to do."

Conversation by seniors haunted us.

"Ever walked on live coals in your bare feet?"

"They clip a strip of hair off right across the top of your head."

"Ever eat fishworms? They taste like nothing you ever ate before. Gosh, they're awful. I can still taste them."

Initiation came on the first Saturday in October. The date approached with dreadful swiftness. At night, in the dormitory, you would hear the terrified sound of someone feverishly praying in a whispering voice on the edge of sobbing. You knew he was fervently seeking a miracle of deliverance. Death, perhaps.

Otto was always asking, "W-w-w-what will they do?"

His obsessive concern came to light in strange ways. Father Bernard was a hearty man dedicated to bringing life to Latin. He flourished the language as if it were scored by John Philip Sousa, and lived the Gallic Wars with gusto.

"And what was Caesar's greatest problem?"

His index finger snapped like a field marshal's baton.

"You, there, Otto."

Otto wriggled from the seat.

"Initiations, Father."

Later he made a mistake in saying publicly, "I hope they don't use any electric stuff. It scares me silly. I got a bad shock when I was about seven or eight, and since then, I'm really scared of it. One more time and I could die. I know that."

This only inspired the tormentors.

"What's that?" demanded Otto, one day in the gymnasium.

A group of seniors were huddled over a strange object on the basketball court. We drifted around the gymnasium, just like prison inmates in the movies, trying to appear casual.

"They can't do it. They can't do it. It'll kill me," screamed Otto.

The object of his fear was a simulated electric chair. It was terrifyingly realistic.

"Oh, no—no!"

"What's with him?"

"He's scared, that's all."

"Oh, yeah, who says?"

"I do. He had a bad fright from electricity when he was small."

Two or three of the other older boys appeared reasonable, but a big fellow, anxious to stem the tide of opinion, turned on me.

"You're a hayseed lad, tryin' to get sympathy for the little mouse. It simply won't work—you farmer, you."

Fists flew, and the disciplinarian separated us, demanding an explanation. He listened and looked at the chair.

"That's enough to frighten anyone. Otto isn't to be put in it, or any electrical gadget used in his initiation."

The priest went away. The boys shrugged their shoulders. Otto looked relieved.

"Well, then," hissed the big fellow, "I'll get Red for this. We'll fry the hayseed."

Nothing can compound misery and loneliness like cultivating new enemies. Sleepless in the early morning I heard, filtering through the cobwebs of sleep, the call of wild geese. The honking migrants were soaring somewhere above the city, and their calls were to echo and re-echo in my lonely, frightened heart.

"Gosh," murmured one student, "wouldn't it be great to go home? They'll be doing the late threshing and Mom will be up making all that good grub. I can just smell the kitchen."

Heads popped up from gray blankets at that, and we must have looked like a group of listening woodchucks when the prefect came out of his room. He stood for several minutes with his hand poised to ring the bell, letting the sound of the geese seep into his own consciousness.

"Lonesome, isn't it?"

He muttered it before the bell shattered the moment with its rude clanging, and the magic evaporated. Yet it remained to haunt me throughout a day enameled with bright sun and the lacquered brilliance of the colored leaves and the exhilaration of wine-spiced air.

"It just seems too nice a day to be cooped up in a classroom."

Father Clem said it and the statement startled me. I had just assumed that people in the city never had feelings about nature. Here in this conglomeration of buildings, in the center of the haphazard city, a city-bred man felt, too, the bittersweet of fall. He was looking out the window as he said:

> *"Tears, idle tears, I know not what they mean,*
> *Tears from the depth of some divine despair*
> *Rise in the heart, and gather to the eyes,*
> *In looking on the happy autumn fields*
> *And thinking of the days that are no more."*

Tough boys, happy boys, sad boys, big boys, and little ones were impaled for a moment on the searching intense point of the quotation. But youth has a strange sensitivity which it tries ardently to disguise. So that day the rugby field and the tennis and handball courts rang with unnaturally loud shouts and a forced kind of laughter. Leaves, raked and piled so carefully, became sites for fierce scrimmage battles, much to the concern of the grounds-keeper. There were pranks galore. Everyone was covering up.

Yet, the memories came back. I was standing in the diamond-cut light of early morning on the way from dormitory to chapel when my English teacher passed. He took a deep breath, coughed a little as the fresh air hit lungs which were more used to cigarette smoke, and said:

> "*I saw old autumn in the misty morn*
> *Stand shadowless like silence, listening*
> *To silence.*"

He moved off before I could reply. I sensed his friendship. A frustrated writer, he had started to encourage me after seeing my first composition. He spoke of the power and dignity and majesty of words. In classroom he was formal and academic, but when we were alone he was different.

We who came from the country drifted easily toward remembrance. The hills of our homes swam into consciousness dappled with color and we saw the mist of drifting smoke from autumnal fires and kitchen chimneys. We lived on the edge of sadness in autumn.

Then there came a day when the sun was tardy in coming up, obscured by clouds and grayness that raced and played across the skies as the wind flung cold rain in haphazard directions. Now and again the sun would peek through, but the clouds, the splattering rain, and the mixed-up light and darkness gave chaotic and turbulent impressions.

The golden days were over. As we finished the final study period that night, Father Ruth rang down the curtain by saying:

> *"The windy flights of autumn flare;*
> *I watch the moonlit sails go by;*
> *I marvel how men toil and fare;*
> *The weary business that they ply;*
> *Their voyaging is vanity,*
> *And fairy gold is all their gain,*
> *And all the winds of winter cry,*
> *My love returns no more again."*

To add insult, our initiation, after being postponed, happened on a sparkling fall day. The original day of gusting rain had been discarded because of the visit of educational authorities. On the morning of doom, four husky lads surrounded my bed.

"Every one of you freshmen gets a number. Yours is twelve. We'll paint it on your forehead and don't you dare rub it off."

We were animals destined for slaughter under a numerical system. "I'm glad you're following me," said Little Otto, who had been dubbed eleven, "because then you can look after me if I die or something. If it's too awful, go easy on my father because he had a heart attack last year."

It may seem ridiculous now, but it really was awesome for the initiates at the time. Wearing old clothes, we had had to act like babbling idiots in the streets of New Gordon. That was over and now we were like condemned men on the morning of execution. Certainly the Lord was assailed by fierce prayers of intercession that morning in chapel.

"Tell me a saint who helps people," whispered Otto.

"St. Jude," suggested a senior. "He's for hopeless cases."

Tom, a second-year boy, with whom I played tennis, said, "Look, don't be afraid. All they're trying to do is scare you. It's just bluster and bluff."

We had become friends and Tom had introduced me to Galsworthy. We were also junior librarians, and had found a treasure trove of books in the back of the library. These were not given out for general circulation. They were to become one of the most influential parts of my education.

"Oldest clothes possible. Everybody put on rags that are useless. Something you can be buried in."

There have probably been initiations ever since Stone Age man decided to form the Cave Club to keep the women out, and they all have their own mumbo-jumbo. We knew that anticipation was the worst part, but our imaginations overbalanced our reason.

"It has often struck me as incongruous," said a teacher surveying us, lined up in the gymnasium in precision, "really incongruous! How is it that college students who appear to be lacking in any sense of order or organization can set up an initiation with the precision of a military organization?"

There was a hidden trap door in the floor of the gym and number one vanished into the depths of the building. Common sense should have told us that it led to the unused swimming pool, but it seemed like a door to Hades. Diabolically, horrible screams wafted up to our ears. By the time number three was being led away, the conducting officers coming out of the hole in the floor had what appeared to be the blood of human sacrifice splattered on their aprons. When number eight was called, Otto fainted.

"Oh . . . my god . . . my god," he gurgled, and slid to the floor.

The school disciplinarian, posted on the upper running track of the gym, disqualified Otto. Nine and ten promptly fainted but were pronounced to be faking and were pushed limply into the mysterious hole.

"Number twelve."

The trip in darkness was a tormented, faltering affair. Once I was scrambling across the coal in the bins beside the furnaces. I recognized the damp, soapy smell of the shower rooms. Then there was an agonizing crawl along what felt like an outside ledge of the building, but which turned out to be the edge of the swimming pool. Then the ledge ended in thin air and I fell on a pile of gym pads. It was stage-managed so well that I firmly believed I was plunging to my death.

There were worms to eat. Imagination made you think for a short while that the slippery chunks of cold, boiled macaroni dripping with olive oil, were truly worms. I was ducked in ice water, doused in whitewash, and finally sprayed with warm water. I was threatened with what they called a prison haircut, and when I didn't protest they snipped off a forelock that was really an unruly cowlick.

An oversized junior fought to save his mane of curly black hair and ended up looking as if his scalp had been gnawed by rats. One boy, fighting against the simulated fall from a great height, missed the gym pads and broke his arm. This dampened the affair, and the last four boys went through without much effort. I suppose everyone was getting tired.

We cleaned up as well as possible for supper. At the table you sensed that something had changed. I fully realized it later while smoking with a senior in the protective shadow of the statue of the founder of the college.

"It's not such a bad place," he said. "You'll like it now that you're one of us. The old place isn't so bad. You'll make friends here you won't forget all your life."

I could relax then and even enjoy the discomfort of the aggressive boy with the gnawed haircut. I was a St. Gerald's boy. This brought three main stresses. Athletics were aimed more at tiring out our animal natures than at helping us master any kind of proficiency. The second stress was study. We were there to study. There was no mistake about that, but many teachers sprayed out knowledge without giving much individual attention. The third presence was religion and God and the atmosphere was charged with it.

The focal point of our lives was the chapel. We struggled up from sleep each morning after the snarling of the bell, shuffled around like dumb prisoners, and doused ourselves with water. Still heavy-lidded, we straggled to the chapel in a semi-conscious state. It was still chilly dawn or the last darkness of night and the candles flared at us like serpents' tongues of flame.

"Heads up . . . come on, wake up, boys . . . put some spirit into those feet. The Lord is waiting for bright eyes and clean minds."

The disciplinarian's tongue lashed and we made for the chapel and prayers and, for those who desired it, Communion. We were caught here because the disciplinarian had a way of checking to see if our spiritual lives were in a healthy enough state to take Communion. If we failed daily Communion, at least we had to go often enough to indicate that the flame of faith wasn't being overcome by the fires of youth.

The place was prayer happy. At noon, we had the Angelus and prayers and blessed, or asked God to bless, the food. Johnny King said the Lord wasn't listening, because the stuff tasted as bad as ever. At supper, we had the Angelus, blessing, and prayers and before going to the dormitory after study period we prayed in the chapel. We were constantly reminded of the Lord and of how necessary it was to work at being Catholics.

We envied a Jewish lad by the name of Isadore Kaminsky, a Presbyterian called Anderson Adair Bowman, and a boy who said he attended something called the Whispering Word of God Tabernacle. He was the luckiest because he went away smirking every Sunday morning, ostensibly for a full day of religion, and came back in time for "Lights Out."

He said he was a fundamentalist. We didn't know what that meant but a day student called Ignatius Phelan, an Irish Pole, said that the fundamentalist caught a bus to the neighboring city of Winchester to see a girl. We wondered how the strange non-Catholic trio was allowed at the school but Johnny King said that it was "a matter of good old-fashioned economics." Kaminsky's father supplied the college with bedding at a discount. Bowman, a rich man's son, had been expelled from an establishment Protestant school in Toronto for putting laxative in the punch bowl at a reunion of grads. We never heard an explanation for the fundamentalist.

Kaminsky spent most of his time in the college infirmary. He knew every trick in the book about illness, and his family was constantly appearing with fruit and candies and buckets of chicken soup. His mother, a sweet woman with a "tic" in her eye, had a habit of waylaying students on the campus and saying, "It's a shame what is happening to my Isadore, now isn't it?" The flick of her eye made them go away confused that a boy's mother could be so involved in chicanery.

Bowman insisted on going to religion class. He didn't have to attend, but he demanded to be allowed in. By Easter time, he had Father Malloy reduced to a state of mumbling defenselessness.

"Let us consider for a moment the scene before Pilate. Jesus stands . . ."

"Father . . . Father Malloy?"

The roly-poly man with the red face would try to ignore Bowman.

"You must consider Pilate . . ."

Bowman would snap his fingers.

"Our Lord had come to earth to . . ."

"Father, what I can't understand is how you say Christ came down to earth to get Himself strung up by a mob."

Father Malloy would bow with grief.

"Bowman, you shouldn't be here anyhow."

"I'm a Christian . . ."

"Debatable . . ."

The priest recognized instantly that he had made a mistake. He would change the lesson, stammer around, and fill out the period by reading a Gospel of St. Paul in Latin which only the novices understood or pretended to know.

Strangely, however, we were St. Gerald's boys. Some indefinable force was forging unity in this most unlikely of places.

Chapter 8

SPORT

———◆———

I had always assumed that sports were supposed to be fun. They seemed a natural outlet for exuberance and good for both body and mind. This is an old-fashioned view, a far cry from the paid gladiators of today suffering broken bones and cumulative injuries for shortened lives, money, and the financial benefit of owners and promoters.

At St. Gerald's we had another sports phenomenon. Faculty boneheads and overly physical students sought to minimize their intellectual deficiencies by creating hysteria over sports. To them it was a general disgrace for a student not to star in several sports. In this way St. Gerald's, along with most educational institutions, managed to produce its fair share of ill-educated graduates who upheld a so-called "tradition of sports."

Most of the country boys had played cow-pasture softball in the summer and shinny on pond ice in the winter. This was a limited background at a sports-minded college. We had only the faintest ideas of how organized sports were handled. It was apparent, however, from registration day on, that we were being appraised by the leaders.

"See that fellow with the green pants," whispered Otto, who, because of his size, was able to sidle up and overhear most school gossip; "he's the coach of the football team. He's going to ask you to try out for the team."

I was just as vulnerable as anyone else to the sports hysteria. I didn't know what football was all about, but I sensed that the school disciplinarian was inclined to go easy on boys who made the team. There was also the alluring factor that the team played some games out of the city, and these trips represented a certain freedom.

"Ah, go on. He wouldn't ask me."

"Well, he's going to. Wanta know what he said?"

"Sure, what did he say?"

Otto giggled.

"You won't get mad?"

"No, of course not."

"Said you were an awkward kind of looking plow jockey, but chasing the cows probably made you a good runner."

I flamed and flared all day and most of the night. When the coach stopped me after chapel the next morning, he said "Carrottop," and didn't get a chance to say any more. I socked him.

That was one expression that could bring me to a full fighting pitch. Now I was in real trouble. Father Hady, the big-footed recreation director who walked as if his boots had been half-soled with planks, had one love at college. It was the football team.

"Boyle," he would say after the incident, "you have so much energy in starting fights out of the chapel, maybe you can have enough energy to . . ."

Then he would give me another demeaning task to do. I was doing so much fetching and carrying in my free time that the sight of the football squad practicing made that seem an easy way out. There was, however, the small matter of the coach. I hadn't caused him any real physical harm, but there was still the matter of his pride.

"Why don't you try out for the line?"

It was Otto reporting.

"They're short of players and I heard him say he could use you."

The sight of Father Hady clomping in my direction gave me inspiration. Surprisingly enough, I made the team. The coach didn't mention the fight and he even went to the compromising length of having Little Otto as water boy and mascot. As players, we were all entitled to wear a large green G on our white or gold sweaters. Those sweaters ranked above all distinctions, even academic ones, at St. Gerald's. We swaggered, especially in other towns or cities where the population didn't know who we really were. Largely because there was a shortage of players, I hung on, achieving, at least during the football season, a truce with Father Hady.

I was recruited only once to play hockey, in very unusual circumstances. A mighty tremor had passed through the whole establishment when we were challenged at hockey by St. Timothy's, a nearby Anglican boarding school. For some unknown reason, it was presumed that playing them would be a cinch. The school was really a seminary and we were familiar with the black-clad and ascetic-looking boys who walked around the city looking as if they were in mourning.

"Come on down," gasped Otto, racing to the study hall, "St. Timothy's is here to play *and they're all monsters!*"

It was true. There wasn't an undernourished novice on the field. They had managed somehow to round up a team of hockey players, none of whom weighed less than at least two hundred pounds. The game was pathetic. Our players, who by and large were pretty good (one of them later appeared in the National Hockey League), didn't have a chance with the bruisers.

Father Hady was apoplectic.

"Where did you get those bums? Don't tell me they're training to be Anglican ministers?"

A smooth-faced canon smiled.

"Come now, Father, we can't have religious prejudice here. These are some of our more advanced theology students."

Hady glowered. "How come I've never seen them before? If they're theology students, then I'm a member of the Curia."

The canon twinkled. "Why, Father, we have a seminary, too. Don't you think they'll make good missionaries?"

"The cannibals will never eat anything as tough as they look," replied the priest, surprising all of us who had thought him humorless.

It was a shutout. Fourteen to nothing! Next day there was an emergency meeting in the gymnasium. All the student body was lined up. Father Hady stalked the lines.

"This is an emergency."

Clop-clop went his boots.

"We are playing a return game at St. Timothy's."

Clop-clop.

"We are going to win."

Clop-clop! Clop-clop!

"Do you hear me? We are going to win."

His face was purple.

"I am going to make up a team right now. It may have to be a miracle, but we are going to have a team and we are going to win."

Clop-clop!

"You two fellows can skate, so you play center."

Clop-clop! Clop-clop! Clop-clop!

"Now, I will read out the names of the other players."

He then called out a list of the biggest lads he could find. One of them had never skated before.

"I can't skate, Father."

"You can fight."

This stunned us into submission. The bell called for classes and in Religion 6 Father Hady preached eloquently on the Evils of the Reformation.

The less said about the game the better. It was mayhem, and ended in a tie of 2–2. We had a broken nose reported, two cracked collarbones, and numerous fractured ribs. They took two of the so-called missionaries home on stretchers. Next day the dean of

St. Timothy's and the rector of St. Gerald's decided that there would be no more intercollegiate sports.

Despite our "sports tradition" there was actually little evidence of championship material in any of our teams. It was said the only group with a chance for honors was the checker team. Yet, to judge from the portraits of stiff-looking young men in kitchen cupboard array in the front hallway of the college, it was a place of champions.

"Gosh," said Otto, staring raptly at a showcase of silver plates and cups and engraved shields, "wouldn't it be wonderful to bring back a cup or a plaque and have it shown there when new classes come here?"

Because he was shy of being five feet tall, he searched diligently for evidence of midget players.

"See there," he said, peering owlishly at a photo hanging well over his head, "see, there was a player no bigger than I am."

I didn't have the heart to tell him that it was the mascot.

"Boy," he exclaimed as we moved back to the dormitory, "would my family ever be surprised! I'd just love to go home and show them I was a member of a championship team."

Otto was the youngest and the smallest of an oversized and overactive family. He was caught in the dilemma of being proud of them and, on the other hand, resenting their collective attitude about his size.

"You should meet my sister Hannah," he said to me, after he had just received a two-dollar bill in the mail from her. "Boy, is she strong! She's a switchboard operator at the local telephone office, and of course all the salesmen who come to town try to get funny with her."

He was beside himself with amusement.

"The switchboard was in a room behind the old barroom at the hotel, and this fellow, Bert Smith, who traveled in harness, was always trying to get her to go to Wiarton to the moving pictures. Finally, she said she would. They saw the movie and then went to the drugstore for a soda. On the way home, he stopped the car, and she broke his arm. Boy, she is sure funny."

I made a resolve to keep as far away as possible from Hannah Alberts.

"But, Otto," I asked, "didn't she break your teeth?"

He nodded.

"She and my sister Liza were tossing me in a blanket and the telephone rang while I was up in the air and she let go of the blanket and ran to answer it. I hit the porch railing and got my two front teeth knocked out."

Stronger boys than myself shuddered at the thought of the Alberts family. We heard that his brother Hugh once shouldered six hundred-pound bags of flour and carried them twice around the race track during the Dominion Day celebrations. His brother James was reported to have broken a man's jaw with one poke of his fist; the unemployed transient tried to hold up the Alberts' butcher shop and ended up in the hospital.

Otto was so determined to surprise his family by making his mark as an athlete that, he began a novena. He haunted the chapel besieging heaven with prayer, seeking divine intercession to help him participate in sports. The rest of his spare time was spent haunting the playing field or the gymnasium where the various teams were being formed.

At first, he was ignored. Then a kind of pity became evident.

"Want to stand in?" asked the baseball coach.

Otto was delighted, and five minutes later, trying to catch a fly ball, he collided violently with the high, red board fence and knocked out the two false front teeth. He put them in his pocket and went on as if nothing had happened.

We went to the "Bull Driver's" class. That was an irreverent name for a very learned and academic teacher who was trying his best to interest us in *Religio Medici,* comments by Sir Thomas Browne on Christian morals. He had a habit of walking up and down in the classroom, swishing a ruler, and barking questions at the class.

"Alberts—Otto, that is—where were we yesterday?"

The little fellow stood up and the words slithered out, swishing and sibilant. The teacher turned in utter amazement and then said, quoting from Browne's "Letter to a Friend," without a single change of expression, " 'The Egyptian mummies that I have seen, have had their mouths open, and somewhat gaping, which affordeth a good opportunity to view and observe their teeth, wherein 'tis not easy to find any wanting or decayed: and therefore, in Egypt, where one Man practised but one operation, or the diseases but of single parts, it must needs be a barren profession to confine unto that of drawing teeth, and little better than to have been tooth-drawer unto King Pyrrhus, who had but two in his head.' "

Then he pointed a dramatic finger at the gaping-mouthed lad and bellowed, "Go, in the name of the Almighty and have that gap fixed in your mouth!"

Otto had his teeth replaced. They had been in sockets. The New Gordon dentist worked a bridge arrangement. Three days later he managed to get into a basketball game and he lost the bridge. His sports career was getting expensive and so he tried a new dentist and a return to the socket idea. In a handball game, the teeth were knocked out again. This time one of the janitors tried a bit of homemade dentistry. It didn't work very well, and he whistled when he talked.

We discovered then a humane approach that we didn't know existed at the college.

"Otto," said the dean, in a special interview, "we are aware of how you have tried out for various sports and are deeply sympathetic that your teeth seem to always end up as casualties."

He shuffled the papers on his desk.

"Now, you must realize that the present teeth are causing some difficulty in the classrooms, and so we will arrange to have you go to the school dentist at no cost to yourself."

He paused.

"There is one condition. You will not play in any more strenuous games. We are aware of your desires, and I have arranged to make you an assistant coach of the football team. You will be expected to help carry water and make yourself generally useful."

He smiled.

"This will, of course, mean you will appear in the group picture."

Otto was overjoyed. He gave full credit to the novena, evidently not realizing just how distracting a gaping mouth or whistling teeth had been in various classrooms.

None of us said anything, but were more inclined to give credit to Divine Providence when the "Bull Driver" was transferred to an administrative post. It seems the college administrators hadn't known about the *Religio Medici* being taught, and since it was in praise of the Reformation and since this was long before ecumenism, the book was considered unsuitable. It didn't really matter. None of us understood what he was teaching, anyway.

But sports were not finished with Little Otto. He became one of the most popular students in the place. Like so many small people, he was useful. He was just the size to squeeze behind the library stack and overhear what the faculty was talking about in the board room. He was also small enough to crawl out the coal chute and slip downtown for refreshments when midnight famine threatened us.

"I'll say one thing for the little guy," said Johnny King, bestowing an accolade, "he doesn't squeal. Those black robes in the front office have been trying to get him to become a stool pigeon, but he never opens up."

Otto also had a supply of salami sent to him from time to time by his family. We considered this, along with a special kind of chocolate biscuit with a marshmallow center (sold as a loss leader by a local chain store), and soda pop to be the essential ingredients for wonderful snacks. They were especially good when consumed in a shelter of blankets spread over exercise bars in the gymnasium. The combination also produced nightmares.

Now the "seeing-eye mouse" came under a mysterious protective code. Bullies stopped trying to tease him. Arrogant ones even seemed to be trying to get admitted to the ring of his friendship. We ignored them, except on the famous occasion when the whole school had to be called in to save the honor of Otto Alberts.

Having functioned more or less as mascot and water boy for the football team, Otto had written about his appointment as assistant coach, hoping to impress his mother and father and the legendary family of enormous brothers and sisters. He dreamed that they might see him in his glory, wearing a sweater, five sizes too large, but sporting a letter G.

"Trouble is," he said, "they don't pay much attention to football up our way. It's not much of a game. Some of the Italian section hands boot around a ball a bit on Sundays, but hockey is what my folks are really interested in."

We had some doubts about prayer. It never seemed to help us with tough examinations, but Otto must have had a private pipe line to the angels. Else, why would his family get the idea that Otto was really playing hockey! Furthermore, why would they all decide to come down to New Gordon to watch him in action?

"I'm in a terrible mess," he said, "it's dreadful. They're coming down Saturday night and they wonder if there'll be a match. My dad is even closing up his butcher shop that night. That's something, because that's the best night for business."

Otto had, of course, tried hockey, but his teeth and his size were enormous handicaps. There was also the rector's ban.

"Gosh, Otto, maybe you better be sick."

He shook his head.

"No good. All my mother would have to do would be to take one look at me and she would know I was faking. No use at all."

We repaired to Johnny King's. He had a private room because he was older and had money. He also had a crystal set in his clothes closet where, if you were specially favored, you might be asked over to listen to radio broadcasting, a novelty of the time which most of us didn't think would amount to much.

Johnny sucked on his pipe. He was allowed to smoke his pipe

in private and we smoked along because his pipe was a wonderful disguise when he didn't have any ideas. It gave an impression of thought. We didn't know what to do. Finally Johnny made an announcement.

"Otto is going to play on Saturday night."

"But, those guys from Winchester will murder him."

King glared. He had a sense of command, later proved in the U. S. Marines.

"We'll do a little persuading in their dressing room before the game. This is what is known as the softening-up process."

Most of us had doubts, although Johnny was a man of action. But Otto was still depressed.

"I'll make a fool of myself. Why, my *sisters* are as good as any players on the team."

Mr. and Mrs. Alberts and the family of eight arrived. The awesome switchboard operator couldn't be there, but wrote to Otto that she would call from time to time to see how it was going. Long distance was free for her in emergencies.

A history of Canadian hockey would be incomplete without the story of this game. The Alberts family were escorted to the rink and the students of St. Gerald's paid the Winchester team ten dollars to throw the game, after threats from our bigger players had failed and had seemed certain to cause a brouhaha. Money was the only form of softening-up they understood.

Otto played center. The first puck was dropped and he swiped at it and fell down, but he was somehow picked up and actually worked on the end of Johnny's hockey stick and pushed, puck and all, into the Winchester goal. The rest of the period was mere confusion, but somehow either Otto looked good or everyone else was so bad that he gained stature by comparison.

"Say," said his father, after the first period, beaming and inviting everyone up to his village for a weekend, "that Otto is a marvel. I just never thought he had the size for it. Where does he get it?"

"We put weights in his shoes," said Johnny.

In the second period, the forwards of St. Gerald's developed a clever system of keeping Otto between them, and the referee never seemed to notice the offsides it produced. But he noticed everything that even began to look like an offense on the part of the Winchester team. Johnny King had to interfere to keep him from sending them all to the penalty box at the same time.

The score was eight to two for St. Gerald's in the last period when our team decided to let Otto shine on his own. An opposition player lost his temper, forgot about the bargain, and took a swipe at Otto as he set off alone for the Winchester goal. He knocked the little fellow down and the nine members of the Alberts family hopped the boards and literally charged the ice.

It took the rector and the whole administrative staff to clean up the mess. They had been puzzled anyhow by the whole thing because it had been considered prudent not to let them in on the secret. Our entire hockey team was put on notice to be punished but the charges were dropped after a private meeting between the rector and Johnny King.

The Alberts family had a great time, particularly enjoying the open fight. But were they taken in?

Otto, who lost his front teeth again in the fight, said they were. That's all that really mattered. Mr. Alberts, on the other hand, dropped in one day with a salami for each member of the team and winked when he said, "This is a little present from Otto for his wonderful teammates. He'll probably never find such grand fellows again as long as he lives. Now I just want you to know if you or your families ever want meat wholesale, you just come up to see me at the Alberts' Meat Shop, and I want to tell you I make the best sausages in the country."

He did too!

Chapter 9

ESCAPE

———◆———

St. Gerald's College was cheap and efficient. It was Depression time and the college gave an opportunity for education to many who otherwise could not have afforded one. The teachers we regarded as misfits, were, in retrospect, dedicated men, and several were quite amazing.

But there were horrors. I can't, for instance, forget THE WALK on Sunday afternoons. We were allowed out in pairs on a Saturday afternoon. But on Sundays the pairs made up into groups. Each group had a leader, a black-clad seminarian, who must have been assigned the job as penance. Each group of twelve shaped up beside the gymnasium building at two o'clock, Sunday afternoon. "The Death March!" Someone had shouted that on the first Sunday, and the name stuck in spite of the disciplinarian's lecture.

"Gentlemen, you are representative of your school, and you must act with proper deportment to uphold the standards of this school. Most of you are new here, but in time you will have an affection for your alma mater. This is to be your home for the next few years. Here is where the formation of your character will begin with educational and spiritual help from the teachers. Be proud of your school and act so that your school will be proud of you. No more nonsense. Fresh air and discipline will help you."

We formed up silently and at intervals marched off toward

Main Street. The plan was to go along to Queen Victoria Street, then swing down to the park and rest for a time beside a small artificial lake. Then we marched back to Main Street, swung past the cathedral and the cemetery and railroad tracks, and arrived back at the college.

Today, New Gordon is a busy, industrial center. Then it was a stagnated depressed place, identical with hundreds of others in Western Ontario, lower Michigan, or upper New York State. They were dominated by countless churches of a bewildering variety of denominations, and puritanism was manifest on Sundays. On Sundays the only other busy place besides the churches was the bootlegging establishment, which everyone knew about. There were no organized sports. Theaters were closed. The Greek restaurants were open, but they were dull places, uniformly trimmed with Vitrolite. The Chinese cafés were open, too, and they were dingier and friendlier, but most of them sold bootlegged whisky in teapots and were out of bounds. The hotels, which depended during workdays on commercial travelers, were like morgues on Sundays. A few old men sat in their lobbies and smoked or aimed at spittoons.

We were forbidden on pain of expulsion to even set foot in a hotel! This meant that during each term at least one student would go "stir crazy," and rent a room at a hotel. He would throw a party, and, sooner or later, he couldn't resist the temptation to telephone an invitation to one of the teachers. Within days we were lined up in the study hall and he was drummed out, usually in absentia. Common sense had told him to beat it before the retribution. The formal expulsion was simply to scare hell out of the rest of us.

Townspeople, bored on Sundays, lined up to watch our march; it gave them something to do. As for us, we did our best to coax the leader to allow us at least to visit a soda fountain.

"Can we stop and get something at the Greek's?"

Stony silence.

"Father . . . oh, excuse me . . ."

That was the old trick of the army recruit giving a corporal higher rank.

"Wouldn't you like a banana split?"

The novices were constantly fasting and so the poor fellow usually gave in. The ice cream parlor afforded the privacy of booths. Nick, a voluble, spitting, fat Greek, was smart enough to give the leader a place behind the artificial palms. On the other side of the restaurant girls sat in individual booths. This was a mystery. We were, with the exception of the rich South Americans, certainly no prize for any girl. Yet, the girls attempted continually to make dates.

"It's simple," explained Johnny King, "they know you're not supposed to have dates. You know you're not supposed to. They try for the same reason you do. Because it's forbidden, and it's Sunday in this damn dull place."

Nick was helpful. He carried notes back and forth on the trays.

"Meet me behind the post office tomorrow afternoon at four o'clock."

"I'll get out the side entrance at ten tomorrow evening."

We were enthralled by the illicit nature of the affair. It broke the monotony, and yet we were frightened stupid of even trying anything.

We may have dreaded the conducted Sunday afternoon walks, but it was nothing compared to the fear the local merchants had of the affair. Their horror increased proportionately as the boys grew adept at minor vandalism. These were really reprisals, because we felt the local people looked down their noses at us as if we were prison inmates let out for exercise. Comments from the bystanders made that clear:

"When did you break jail?"

"Still on bread and water?"

"Where's the hanging?"

"Does your mother know you're out?"

You were helpless. Caught replying with a rude and obscene remark, you were put on detention; and at St. Gerald's detentions were rigid. You might also be sent to the front to march ahead of the chaperones like a "Judas goat" to a slaughter yard. But like old "cons" we managed some unusual things.

"Oh, gosh, look at that."

Somebody on point duty called it out. The pack straggled to a stop in front of the Bijou movie theater, silent on Sundays, but displaying photographs of the latest attraction.

"It's the picture about Knute Rockne."

The leader would trip back to see what was wrong.

"Can we look at the pictures?"

"Please, let's see it."

"Come on, it won't take a minute."

Usually he weakened and walked away, demonstrating disdain for such petty and earthly distractions. The students swarmed like a pack of hungry locusts in a grain field. They kept an anxious eye on the novice and then, without being called, moved off to follow him. They didn't want him to look back. I have seen every poster and placard and photograph stripped from a lobby in a matter of seconds. What is more, there would not be a trace of one on a single student.

On Mondays the trouble always erupted.

"Students who have material from the movie theaters will please leave it at the table in the center hall. No recriminations if it is turned in, but if it happens again there will be punishment."

The stuff, or practically all of it, would somehow appear for the theater manager and the red-faced policeman to take away. Then, a mysterious thing happened. Most of it vanished again the next night from the theater. The theater manager, accompanied by the same policeman, would come to assembly after lunch.

"But," the disciplinarian fussed, "the boys have not been out since yesterday."

That was true. St. Gerald's was a fortress, and discipline was iron clad. There was not a sign, in the case of the *Four Horsemen of Notre Dame* movie, of a placard or photograph for all the time it was running locally. Then you started to see pictures pasted up on the inside of lockers or posters hanging on the walls of the private rooms. The mystery was left undisturbed. Most of our teachers had graduated from the same institution. They knew the answers.

But no one knew the answer to the case of the missing traffic signs. For weeks, traffic signs such as STOP and GO kept vanishing from downtown. These were big signs, and they couldn't be smuggled away under coats. The college was mustered. No one pleaded guilty. The place was searched. Nothing was found.

One day Little Otto confided to me that his favorite uncle was the one-man police force in a small Ontario village where the council was too miserly to buy him any signs. Otto had arranged to trade salamis from his father's butcher shop with a street sweeper who trundled the signs up in his cart and stored them in a vacant room behind the boilers. Since the janitors never bothered to clean except where directed, the cache was secure.

"I didn't know how I was going to get them up to him, but I figured that if I got the signs, some way would come to me."

He didn't consider it stealing because as he said, "Everybody in the school knows taking souvenirs isn't stealing."

For once the full college spirit, which the staff tried so desperately to encourage without result, arose spontaneously. Clandestine meetings of all kinds flourished. More effort went into the affair than students devoted to all of their academic studies. For four dollars the garbage collector smuggled the signs to a drover who trucked livestock to a local packing plant. The drover, a cousin of Otto's, simply picked the stuff up at a prearranged spot and took it along to Otto's uncle. For many years the village retained an overabundance of traffic signs. The villagers, of course, disregarded them. But they were pleased with them until the initials "N.G.P.D.," indicating New Gordon Police Department, were interpreted by some busybody as an attempt to bilingualize the sturdy hamlet which prided itself on its United Empire Loyalist stock. The council ordered them removed at once.

I had assumed that the notes exchanged at the Greek's were sheer bravado. It was a shock to realize that, in spite of the system, the rules, and the vigilance, some boys were actually going out on dates.

"There's something funny here," suggested Otto one afternoon in the gymnasium.

It was a free period, supposedly for sports and recreation following classes and preceding the evening meal. With rain drizzling outside, the gym was crowded. Just then, Mel, the squat moneylender, came along. He slipped each one of us a free cigarette, a noteworthy event in itself, and said, "Come on, fellas, make a fuss here. Squabble over the handball or something."

We did and the sports director came to ask what was wrong. We didn't know what to say, but it simmered down. Mel waved from the other side of the building, indicating he was happy. Otto was suspicious, however, and moved up to the track that ran around on the upper level overlooking the courts and looked out of the screened windows to the street side.

"Look there," he nudged me, "look at those fellows."

Two men, who appeared to be priests, had somehow materialized on the street from nowhere, unless it was from the building we were in.

"They don't walk like priests. They're not."

Mel had followed us.

"Not so loud," he hissed, "you want those fellows to get caught?"

We were ushered secretively past the unused swimming pool to a door with no outside handle. Mel produced one, turned the knob, and we went into a small storage room. There was Lennie, a lean, matchstick fellow who always seemed to need a shave. He glowered.

"What did you bring those guys for?"

Mel tried to placate him.

"They made a fuss when I was slipping Pete and Eddy down here."

Lennie wanted to keep everything from us, but Otto showed his spunk.

"Look, what are you up to? We're not going to tell, but if somebody questions us, we're liable to give you away without knowing we are."

"You're right," volunteered Mel. "You see, we needed a place to keep our stock and so we rented the room from the engineer and he gave us the knob to the door. He doesn't think any of the staff know this room exists."

Mel and Lennie were our resident Shylocks. They were the ones who loaned money, rolled and sold cigarettes, bought clothing and trinkets, swiped examination papers, and did other useful work for the student body. In this case, they helped would-be Romeos. I was stupid but Otto divined the answer.

"Disguise, that's it. You guys rent disguises for students."

Lennie was proud of his ingenuity. He produced a stock of black bibs attached to collars that buttoned on backward. With a soft, black felt hat, they rented at twenty-five cents an occasion, if you didn't dirty the collar. It was fifty cents if the collar was soiled. You had to wear a dark suit to make the outfit effective.

"It's a very good deal," said Mel, "we get you in and out of the college and rent you the outfit."

"But," said Lennie, glowering, "there are a few rules. This is a secret society. You'll have to be initiated into it now that you've found us out."

Otto paled.

"No . . . no . . . we won't tell."

He was paralyzed at the thought of a secret society, his grandmother having filled him with tales of terror at freemasonry initiations. Mel was inclined to let us go but Lennie was having no part of a possible security leak.

We struck a bargain. We would take the oath, but we didn't have to go through all the horrible details of the initiation. The light was extinguished and by candlelight we proceeded to recite, "By the holy powers of his satanic majesty, I am now a slave to silence, promising that for a period of five years I will not reveal one detail of the Mel and Lennie escape route plan. As a token of my pledge, I now donate my blood, which shall be mingled with that of my fellow pledgers."

At this point, Mel scratched our hands with a pin and a few drops of blood were put in a rather dirty-looking sealer.

"Do you swear on what you hold most precious, your life?"

"I do swear on my life."

Mel blew out the candle and in the darkness Lennie said, "The penalty of breaking the oath is held in the hands of Satan, who may at any time do what he will with you."

Then Mel added, "Amen," in a final, chilling, if incongruous way.

We went back to the dormitory, afraid to speak to each other. The priest in the study hall made us dab Mercurochrome on the scratches after trying without success to find out where they came from.

I had a terrible dream that night as a character with a tail chased me with a red-hot pitchfork. In the light of next day, we had the thrill of knowing we were now charter members of the Mel and Lennie escape route and for twenty-five cents could purchase a few hours of illicit freedom. It was comforting, even if we were too chicken to try it.

Chapter 10

FOREIGNERS

———◆———

Growing up not too far from the United States-Canada border, but with Lake Huron solidly between me and them, I had strange ideas about the United States. First of all, Detroit was a very big city that revolved around a man called Henry Ford. He was paying what seemed a fortune for workers.

"Five dollars a day."

It lured many of our local lads who since World War I hadn't been too satisfied with conditions. Some enjoyed a first taste of independence from their families. They came back for holidays with new cars, straw hats with colorful bands, wonderful neckties, and money to spend. It was fantastic. A man said he stood in the same place all day and twisted four nuts on four bolts as the engines came by on an endless belt.

"Monotonous," he said, "sure, it gets monotonous, but look at the money I make."

I imagined a large tract of land north of Detroit where lumberjacks worked all winter and in spring came down the rivers to spend their money and get in trouble at such places as Saginaw and Bay City. This could be attributed to my grandfather, who embellished stories of his lumbering days with loving dreams.

I knew about the Mississippi River from Mark Twain. The Maitland River meandered through the back of our farm. On a

homemade raft on our river, I yearned for the sound of a steam-
boat around the bend, settling for the perfunctory "toot" of the
tannery whistle of Clover at lunch time and closing.

That was the total of my knowledge of America and Americans.

I anticipated meeting Americans at St. Gerald's College with a
certain fear. On my first day, after I had bloodied the nose of the
bully who was teasing Otto, I was warned.

"Bill is an American," someone whispered.

"So what?"

"So, they stick together and *they'll get you.*"

Shades of 1812! I tried to sleep, tortured by visions of them waiting to beat me up. I was wary on the way to chapel and distracted
during prayers. Then an American approached me.

"You the fella that beat up on Big Bill?"

"Yeah!"

He smiled.

"He deserved it. All last year he pestered the smaller boys and
some of us were going to gang up on him, but you really took him
by surprise."

"You mean . . . you're not . . . ?"

"A friend of his? Of course not. Sure, we're all from the United
States but that blowhard makes us all ashamed."

I relaxed. "Where are you from?"

"Port Huron. My father has a farm about twenty miles from
Port Huron."

A farm! This was staggering news.

"I suppose you must be on the edge of the timber line?"

He looked as if I had lost my mind.

"Timber line? It's miles and miles before you get to any timber."

"But the lumber woods . . ."

"Pretty well gone. There's a lot away up in the Michigan penin-
sula but I've never been up there."

I kept quiet. There were other surprises.

"This is George Rawle," said Little Otto, adding almost breathlessly, "He's from Montana."

He was a lean, tanned youngster with a shock of sandy hair and all my ideas of Zane Grey and *Riders of the Purple Sage* came back with a flash of romantic notions.

"Gosh. You really from Montana?"

"Butte. Copper mines there."

"Is your father a rancher?"

"No, my father is a plumber, but I have an uncle who has a ranch. He keeps sheep."

This was an added blow. Somehow, because of my reading, I had been on the side of the cattlemen. Sheepmen and home-steaders, "nesters," brought fences. It was a bitter time for a romantic.

"Say, you're the fellow who was fighting with Big Bill," smiled a round butterball of a boy. "Come on up to my room for a treat. I'm from Detroit. My old man keeps a delicatessen," he said cheerfully. "We're Polish and make the best sausage in the world."

The New Orleans boy with the soft drawl was a scholarship student in religion. A New York boy's father manufactured ladies' underwear. The two boys with the most adventurous backgrounds were from Canada. One of them, from the Ottawa valley, had worked on the log drive because his father was a lumberman. A Swede from Medicine Hat had worked for two years as a cowboy in Alberta to get tuition money.

Everyone was curious about Blinky. He was really Marvin Weber behind enormous glasses. He was studious and didn't say much. That made the other boys even more suspicious, and he seemed to have spending money.

"What does your father do, Blinky?"

"My father doesn't work."

"You mean he's rich?"

"No, he isn't rich."

Blinky looked uncomfortable.

"Look, Blinky, level with us, or you'll get put out of the gang."

"Well, he runs a—a—well, I don't know what to call it."

"He's a bootlegger?"

"He is not."

"He's in a carny throwing crooked games?"

Blinky protested, "He is not."

"Well, what then?"

"He has a turnabout."

Everyone looked mystified.

"Oh, come on. There's no such thing as a turnabout."

"Well," said Blinky finally, "the Depression was pretty awful. My dad tried everything and then he finally hit on this and he has a turnabout."

"How does that keep him from working?"

Blinky looked uncomfortable.

"Our farm is the last one on the side road. The road is narrow. My father set up signs along the road. You know, like saying so many miles to the turnabout."

The boys were impatient.

"Yeah, but what is it?"

"Just that. People driving along the main road see these signs saying how far it is to the turnabout. They get to the corner and it says, 'Only Half Mile to the Turnabout.' They turn down and a quarter mile away the road narrows down with a fence on each side close up and they come to this gate."

"So, what happens, Blinky?"

"My father sits there and he tells them for a dollar they can open the gate and use the turnabout, which is a track in the field. If they don't want to they can back down the narrow road. That's the turnabout."

Blinky escaped in the nick of time.

To a country boy, the city of New Gordon was a noisy, changing place. It was like a July 1 celebration with crowds, clangor, and smells that went on all year. It seemed strange that people could live the year round in such surroundings.

Sleepless one night, I crept out on the fire escape. It was Indian summer and exceptionally balmy. With an almost full moon and the city quiet, the place had an entirely different atmosphere. Cars went along distant streets on whispering tires. Occasionally a door would slam. Voices drifted up in fragments. A yard engine fussed around and grunted past the railroad station. Dogs growled here and there and were silenced by gruff, muffled-sounding commands.

"What are you doing out there?" demanded the prefect.

"Sorry, but I can't sleep."

He stepped out and closed the door after him.

"Don't blame you. It's too nice a night to sleep anyhow."

He lit a cigarette, hesitated, and asked if I wanted one.

"No, thanks."

"It's a wonderful thing to look at a city at night," he said, almost as a soliloquy. "You country lads don't like cities but that's because you don't know them."

"They're too noisy."

"Oh, go on. I'll bet at night there's more noise around your place than here," he said. "Animals and birds and roosters crowing in the morning. Just listen. See over there. St. Mark's Anglican Church. I was born in a house just a block the other side of it.

"My mother didn't want to leave home. She didn't trust hospitals. In fact, my father had to insist she have a doctor. How she loved the city! I can still see her setting out with her basket in the morning to shop, stopping to gossip a bit here and there and make calls on people who were sick or old."

He seemed lost in remembering and I finally asked him why he liked the city.

"It's strange in a way, but living in a city can ease loneliness. You open your door and go out and see and talk to people, or if you want to be alone, you go home and close your door. I like a city in the fall like this when the back streets are covered with leaves and there's a smell of smoke. We liked to go outside after supper in the dark and romp around and pretend we couldn't hear our folks when they called."

Stubbing out the cigarette, he started to go in and then changed his mind.

"I liked walking home at night down the side streets and feeling the cold of late fall and seeing all the houses with the lights on. Children would be huddled at a table studying, the father reading his newspaper and the mother fussing around.

"I suppose," he said, after a pause, "it was always the people. Saying good night to your playmates and then meeting them in the morning and dawdling off to school. Or Saturdays, going to a matinee at the show and having a nickel for popcorn—or flooding along in a crowd going to church on Sunday morning and—oh, well—you better not stay up too late or you'll be asleep in class tomorrow."

He left me, and instead of thinking about what he said, I was suddenly and heartbreakingly lonesome for the valley. I could picture the barn and sheds looking fat and silvery in the moonlight and hear a hound baying at a nocturnal animal in the distance. I didn't hear the city at all. I remembered the soft, gossipy swish of the big pines outside my bedroom and my grandfather stirring in his dreams. Finally I went to bed, more convinced than ever that an education was hardly worth the pain of separation from the familiar.

By Christmas, we at least knew one another. I felt expansive and felt that my father would have been horrified by the thought of anyone having to spend Christmas alone.

"Christmas is a time for charity and sharing," was his motto. "Lonely people should have a chance for a family get-together in this most blessed of seasons."

He didn't say it in such a fancy way as that, but the sentiment was the same. We lived in a semi-remote area and there were very few poor and lonely strangers, especially in the isolation of a cold winter. This was compensated for by Grandfather going to Clover Christmas Eve to meet his cronies, and he usually found a guest. Sometimes, they were shy bachelors without relatives; occasionally, he found real strangers. As a result we had some interesting experiences in connection with charity. One guest came equipped with lice, which he left (or at least a fair number of

them were left behind), and there was a time of great beating
and purifying and burning between Christmas and New Year's.
Another tried to show his appreciation by giving me what might
be called a few fundamental lessons in being a pickpocket. Later
on, dealing with publishers, I wished I had paid more attention.

Now, at school, the fact of the Depression crept into our consciousness. We noticed that the priests now often allowed the
day students to stay for lunch. Some of the boarders dropped out
because they said their parents couldn't afford to let them stay.

"I don't think I'll be back next year," confided Otto. "My father
says he can't collect his bills."

My tuition had been paid. There was little chance to spend my
secret little cache of pocket money, so I could scrape by. But we
all knew the South American students were different. They had
large allowances. They were at St. Gerald's because they had been
expelled from Spanish or Swiss institutions.

Ramon was an Argentinian. He was slim, dark, and quiet. He
never seemed to have more money than the rest of us. He didn't
club with the other South Americans, in fact, he seemed to prefer
North Americans. He joined us in the deception of wearing black
turtle-neck sweaters and reversed white collars to pose as priests
and gain free admission on Saturdays at the local movie house.
This worked until a suspicious manager made a check one Saturday and found more spurious clergymen than paying patrons.

Christmas was something special that year. In spite of my
mother's premonitions, my father had taken over the country
store from my uncle. Father had never been happy farming.
Despite the hard times the lure of the store was too much, and so
the deal was made. I never learned what the deal amounted to.
It was enough that this would be our first Christmas living in the
big white brick house that encircled the store where I had found
such fascination as a visitor and unpaid helper to my uncle in the
past.

Remembering my family's annual search for a Christmas guest,
I wrote them about Ramon. I suppose I overexpressed the

obvious poverty and loneliness of Ramon. They were overjoyed. Christmas of 1931 looked like a winner in every way, with Ramon as our guest.

Christmas Eve was the highlight. Father took an instant liking to Ramon. When he discovered that Ramon's father had a store in Argentina, he felt an instant kinship and introduced him to all the customers.

Being country storekeepers was an experience for us after having lived on the farm, and I was proud of myself for bringing Ramon home. After Mass we had lunch and Ramon broke his reticence and told us about the Posada, which represented the search for Joseph and Mary for a place of refuge until on the ninth day, Christmas Eve, they reached Belen, where Christ was born.

Ramon was a real charmer. When my mother insisted on hanging stockings for both of us, I was mortified. I could just picture the reaction at St. Gerald's College. Ramon was delighted. To him it was a charming custom. For me it was a kind of mortification.

The presents were simple, but Ramon made such a fuss that my mother blushed. By Christmas night I was ready to break his neck.

During the week, at the annual Christmas dance, where I counted on a fair amount of attention from the local girls (being the only boy from our township attending college), I was merely useful in introducing Ramon. It seemed unfair that after I paid his admission to the dance he had the effrontery to have lunch with the one girl I considered my date. I had even confided to him that she was my "steady."

It ended, waiting beside the train in Clover. We had said good-by and there was an awkward moment before climbing the train steps, when Father, who must have been thinking a lot about it, said, "Tell me, Ramon, is your father's store in Argentina anything like ours?"

"Oh, no," he said, taking out a snapshot and handing it to Father, "my father has a business like Señor Macy in New York or Señor Eaton in Toronto. This is the store in Buenos Aires and

he have maybe twenty or thirty like it in all parts of the country.
Please to keep the picture for a souvenir and you must come, all
of you, and have Christmas with us sometime."

I hurried on the train and as we pulled out Father was still staring dumfounded at the snapshot.

Chapter 11

SEX

———◆———

The dissatisfactions of the Christmas holidays were nothing compared to the feelings when St. Gerald's reopened. Loneliness clasped us. It was cold and drab. The first full sense of misery came on a breathlessly cold night when the scream of a locomotive knifed through the sleeping city and invaded our dreams.

"What was that?"

"It's a train."

Commotion surged as the boys came unevenly awake. The lights flicked on and the sleepy prefect complained.

"Oh, come off it. A train? Surely you fellows have heard a train before. Now, back to sleep and no more racket."

The lights went off and we tried to sleep. The trouble was that we had all heard trains before. The sound of locomotives was probably the one thing that all the Canadian students had in common. No matter where we came from, we knew the lure of train whistles. Now the lonesome night wail brought us together in a common bond of aching misery.

"You awake?"

"Yeah."

"You know, I come from Saskatchewan, and I never really missed the place until I heard that whistle. Gosh, you should hear the old flyer when it blows at the crossing on a night when it's way below zero."

His words prompted a collective sigh from the rest of the listeners. We heard a mournful freight shuffling across the city. Someone laughed but the flick of the lights warned us back into silence and individual memories.

For a boy growing up in the isolation of an Ontario valley, trains represented contact with the outside world. Train whistles also seemed to adjust somehow to the circumstances of time and weather—they sometimes even heightened the spirits of the boy who paused to listen.

On soft, drippy spring nights, we heard the whistle as the sound ground-hugged its way under the cloud cover. It matched the feeling of spring and the quivering ground so recently released from the grip of frost. It blended with a sense of growingness in the air. A child in the country was aware of the awakening earth, and the locomotive sound was a benediction.

I enjoyed the gentle, rustling nights of young summer. The world was clothed again with new leaves and green grass. The fields had sprouted crops, and on back stoops and porches farmers smoked and chatted in gentle voices, almost as if they didn't want to disturb nature's handiwork.

"Hear the train blow," my father would say, "blows low in the spring. Soft and low!"

For all of us the train whistle in winter brought memories, and the intimation that our worlds were changing. Intruding on us was the soul-stretching of growing up. We were boys being pulled into adulthood.

Things were desperate at St. Gerald's in that time after Christmas. The hockey team was in a cellar position of such ignominy that only a miracle might help. Prayers hadn't worked, although there had been recourse to that. In school, the leader would stop during morning and evening prayers, half cough apologetically, and say, "And now a special prayer for . . . ahh . . . special considerations affecting the college."

The good Lord remained deaf as far as the Flyers were concerned. They would have been more aptly named the Broken Wings. "Porky" Dumart, who it was rumored had once attended the college (although we didn't believe it), was brought in for a Saturday afternoon game with some other members of the Kraut line of Boston and we were sure that they would give our team enough adrenalin to sparkle. They ended up on the short end of an eight-to-one score!

Faced with such a depressing hockey situation, we began to look for other extracurricular activities. There was, for instance, a concerted attempt to fool the authorities about contact with the other sex; with the full complicity of our parents, they had set out to keep us away from girls.

"Girls are a distraction. Young men with careers in mind and the possibility of being blessed with vocations simply cannot have time for wasting."

That was the substance of the constant propaganda.

"You know something," said Johnny, who was older and had worked very hard to send himself to college, "they're really getting my dander up. It seems to me they're deliberately challenging us to see if we can fool them. Well, I'm going to fool them. You watch and see, and they won't be able to touch me."

Betting ran high. Some, with secret hero worship for King, were certain he could accomplish it. Others believed the disciplinary forces of the school were so well organized that no one could beat them.

"Good old Johnny will make it."

"Listen, there isn't a trick in the book they don't know about. Some of those teachers were experts at skulduggery when they were going to school. I know. My dad told me."

Little Otto was the wisest of all. "He'll win, and he'll use somebody else so he can get away with it."

He didn't elaborate, but we had all overlooked the matter of families. There was a rule that if you had any relatives in the vicinity of New Gordon, they could take you out for Sunday afternoon and dinner. You had to be back before lights-out on Sunday night.

Johnny King was the only decent athlete we had, and because of that, during our rugby season, which was being bastardized into football, he had a certain amount of freedom. This wore off by Christmas and by the middle of winter when hockey was a preoccupation, he had lost most of his edge over the rest of us. Hockey was not an American game and our hockey showing was miserable. That didn't prevent King from scheming to get out.

"How are you going to do it, Johnny?"

"My relatives."

"You have relatives?"

It seemed farfetched, because Johnny had been raised in an orphanage in Ohio, U.S.A.

"Yeah, my relatives are going to ask me out next Sunday."

"Did you know they were your relatives before you came here?"

"No, it was an amazing thing. You remember the time I strained a tendon and was laid up in the hospital?" he grinned.

Everybody remembered that. It was during the football season, and faint hopes of victory dried up when he went to hospital.

"Sure, but what has that got to do with it?"

"That young blond nurse is a King."

"Lots of people are called King."

"Yes, but they're not my cousins."

It was brilliant. We moped for the rest of the week and lamented that we hadn't thought of such a brilliant play. Any idea of expropriating a ruse like that before Johnny did was discouraged, on the premise that we wanted to stay healthy.

On the following Sunday Mr. and Mrs. King arrived and drove Johnny away after lunch. We were watching from every available window as he waved jauntily back to us.

"There's going to be trouble," prophesied Otto. "Their name isn't King. They're no more Kings than I am."

"How do you know?"

"He travels for a spice company. My father buys stuff from him for making sausage. My God, wait until the priests find out."

"Who is he? What's his name?"

"Koenig. Emil Koenig. He's German and the girl's name is Hamilton. She just lives with them."

The gloom of mid-winter faded in the excitement. When it was time for the dreaded Sunday afternoon walk, we shaped up in groups with a pale disciplinarian leading each one. There wasn't a single straggler. Something was bound to happen!

We marched along and came to the Main Street and set out for the park. Just by the English-American Hotel, Johnny King appeared in sight. A blond minx, the same nurse, was walking beside him with her hand on his arm. The disciplinarian, a nearsighted and somewhat studious fellow by the name of Seegmuller, nodded to them and then did a double take.

"You there . . . King . . . what are you doing?"

This was the moment Johnny had been waiting for.

"Just taking a walk."

Seegmuller gasped like a hooked fish, and Johnny left him dangling.

"But . . . but . . . the . . . ahh . . ."

"Oh, excuse me, this is my cousin Maryida. Maryida King," said Johnny, with perfect poise.

The disciplinarian blushed as if frightened by the proximity of a girl and led us away He kept stopping every so often, however, to look back and seemed to be trying to recall something. That night after lights out the dormitory buzzed like a hive of bees.

The Kings called again the following Sunday and we were treated to the same performance. The rector, we later discovered, was now doing a bit of quiet checking and before the third Sunday, Johnny was summoned to his august presence. King was given full marks for ingenuity. The rector would not accept the remarkable similarity between Koenig and King and the fact that Mr. Koenig was also a product of an orphanage. We went back to inventing new ways of breaking winter monotony.

Our custodians recognized the danger signals. Two boys were caught in chapel playing with poker dice. They were hauled before student assembly. "This comes perilously close to *blasphemy!*"

The rector's paunch quivered under his black soutane and the fringed tassel of his sash splayed out dramatically. Peter Tilley and Ned Prevost stood stolidly and contemplated the room. That was another danger sign. If they had been frightened, it would have made more sense, but the black mood of desperation made them incapable of being sorry.

"The Roman soldiers gambled for the bloodstained robe of Our Lord crucified on Mount Calvary."

It would have made more sense to accuse Tony Roncalli, who was a compulsive gambler and placed bets on horses with the baker who delivered pastry to the Tuck Shop.

"In my entire career, I have never heard of such a disgraceful thing. When Father Zader told me, I couldn't believe it. I couldn't believe it," said the rector, taking time out to pause. He was a good speaker. He knew he was a good speaker. He took every opportunity to keep in practice, and this was a golden chance. He whipped out a large handkerchief and blew his nose. Then he mopped his brow. He stabbed at his cassock tail, found the opening nearest his pants pocket, replaced the handkerchief, and folded his hands over his stomach.

"How would it look if I were to write a report to the parents of these two boys and say they had been apprehended while gambling with . . . these . . ."

He picked up the dice gingerly and let them drop on the desk. They clattered into position. A boy near the front of the hall said in a loud whisper:

"A full house—aces and tens."

The faculty broke their inquisitorial board and moved toward the table. Pandemonium broke loose.

"Two bucks says he can't do it again."

"Five bucks he makes a flush."

It was one of those moments even the most masterful of men

couldn't handle. Some faculty members tried to smother grins. The students were past caring. The rector blustered but we were dismissed.

Otto, who found he was small enough to wedge in behind a bookstack in the library and listen at the keyhole of a disused door of the staff room, reported interesting news.

"They're concerned about our animal spirits."

"What do you mean?"

"Well, Father Penny, who is always talking like a farmer, says we're like young stock that has been stabled too long. We need more relaxation."

"I suppose the rector suggested we all run around the track about fifty times."

"How did you know?"

"He would."

Otto grinned.

"Father Penny was earthier than that."

"What? I don't get it."

"Father Penny suggested we should have the chance to meet girls."

"What about the good old saltpeter in the soup?"

"The brother from the kitchen says if we get any more saltpeter, we'll all be sick. There's two or three boys breaking out in a rash already."

"What did the rector say?"

"Hah. He said they must be using poor saltpeter. Anyhow, after a lot of niff-nawing, they agreed to have a social evening with the girls of St. Mary's Academy."

"Wowie!"

The news electrified the institution. St. Mary's was a baronial heap of dirty limestone on the far side of New Gordon, operated by a remote order of sisters. We knew little about it, except that once a year we were regimented to attend a music recital.

"I'm going to be sick," promised Johnny King. "I just can't stand another performance of hearing perfectly good music butchered by those amateurs." The younger students were game for anything. Older students groaned at the announcement.

THE STUDENTS OF ST. MARY'S ACADEMY WELCOME THE STUDENTS OF ST. GERALD'S COLLEGE FOR AN INFORMAL ENTERTAINMENT ON THE EVENING OF MARCH 1. THIS IS TO CONTINUE YOUR CATHOLIC EDUCATION AND PERFECT THE ARTS OF SOCIAL DEPORTMENT. THERE WILL BE REFRESHMENTS.

At breakfast time, Billy Zinger immediately pegged the thing as an orgy . . . a sex orgy.

"Haven't you heard?" he whispered. "They've learned that repressed sex causes more madness than anything else, so before all the girls at St. Mary's and all the boys here turn into raving maniacs, they're going to have a real sex bash. It's like the initiation rites that African tribes have when they let the boys and girls pair off. Kind of a Roman carnival."

Common sense told us that it was impossible, but we were in a mood to believe in anything.

"Do you think he's kidding or does he mean it?" asked Otto. "I wouldn't know what to do."

I was green, but I had good eyesight and our township hall dances at home were pretty gamy affairs that ended up in some hasty weddings. Still, I couldn't really bring myself to feel that the authorities of our institutions were as desperate as Zinger made out.

"Father Hady has been appointed to head the committee for the school," reported Otto, back from his listening post in the library.

This dampened the hopes many of us had for the social. Father Hady was a man completely devoid of humor. His spoonerisms in class were simply a living horror. He dropped them with complete abandon, and when we laughed, he was furious. He couldn't see anything funny about them.

"Some of you think we go to arrange the make funny with the

girls at St. Mary's," he glowered in class the next day. "But I am here for to do what you don't."

Disaster struck. Otto fell asleep at his listening post waiting for a meeting of the board and was apprehended by the sound of his snoring. Fortunately, they didn't suspect he was eavesdropping and he was punished simply for being lazy.

"I found out one thing," he volunteered; "Mother St. John has been named to head the committee from St. Mary's."

"Good God," exclaimed Bill, "she's the one with the mustache."

We had seen her. She was the drill sergeant who ordered the girl charges to look straight ahead, quicken their tempo, and start saying the Rosary when we happened to meet one of their groups on a Sunday outing.

"She's murder," acknowledged Johnny King. "She is plain and simply murder on boys. I think she hates them."

We had also seen Mother St. John during our attendance at a recital, an experience which hardened our approach to St. Mary's. It was a ritualized affair without joy. The recitals were at two o'clock on Saturday afternoons. It was one of our free periods when we could laze around, play games, write letters, or do whatever we wanted. We had very few free periods of a similar nature, and anything that infringed on them was an injustice.

"Tomorrow afternoon," announced the rector, after clanging the bell at supper on Friday, "we will be guests for a delightful musical entertainment at St. Mary's Academy."

A mighty groan arose from the tables of the seniors, veterans of previous years. The rector smiled patronizingly.

"Boys, boys, you will give our new students a wrong impression," he cautioned, with a tightening of the muscles around his mouth. "Don't be unfair. We will leave in the same formations as used during the Sunday walks and I want everyone to be prompt. It's a discourtesy to be tardy."

"What about our free time?" demanded someone in a heavily disguised voice.

"We will see how successful our outing is before making any

promises," smiled the rector unctuously, but with an edge of threat.

We marched to the recital and were ushered into a cheerless auditorium to sit on planks placed across boxes. We sat on one side with our group leaders interspersed like guards. Then the girls marched in and sat on the other side, and their numbers were dotted by sisters who sat like female prison wardens.

The welcome, if you could call it that, was given by Mother St. John. A black-clad battleship, she marched on stage and studiously avoided looking at us or even making mention of our presence. A procession of shy girls in navy blue skirts down to their ankles marched on to play the piano, sing, or scratch on violins. For three hours we were numbed in mind and body.

Now with the humorless Father Hady and the forbidding Mother St. John in charge, we were to be exposed to "entertainment." But some were desperately optimistic about the whole thing.

"It may be fun and it's in the evening, anyhow, and we would just be standing around here or sitting in study hall. When you get up close some of those girls may not look too bad."

We marched off during an evening when winter was fighting a rearguard action against spring with blustery winds and squalling snow.

"Maybe there'll be dancing!" suggested Otto, but this was foolishness because it was during Lent.

"Nah," countered Johnny King, "there'll be some kind of games. Silly damned games that Father Hady and that sister thought up. We'll probably have to stay on separate sides of the room. You wait and see."

Just the same, there had been considerable preparation for the event. Fuzz and down had been scraped from boyish cheeks and we were drenched in an amazing variety of scents and potions.

"Whew," snorted Father Penny, inspecting us in our own gymnasium before we started. "This smells like sheep-dipping time."

He poked me in the ribs and whispered, "Those girls won't have a chance against a bunch like you fellows."

"My God, look," exclaimed Johnny King, when we arrived in the auditorium at St. Mary's. "Look at this, would you?"

The room had been transformed by pink and white tissue paper into a frothy palace. The girls were wearing dresses and we stampeded to where they sat on benches in the center of the room. It seemed too good to be true.

Otto was the first to spot the drawback. "Look at the walls," he hissed in a warning voice, "just look at them."

Ranged around the four walls of the auditorium were parents. They sat in pairs, and at that moment I sensed what the early Christians felt when they were driven into Roman amphitheaters.

"First of all, there will be a spelling bee," announced Mother St. John. Father Hady was the spelling master. Some difficulty arose from his pronunciations of the words, and Mother St. John was obviously angry when St. Gerald's won the match.

"Since we are acting as hosts," she said through clenched teeth, her mustache quivering with rage, "I suppose the least we can do is accept the verdict. But for your information, Father Hady, there is no word—*shyllogism.*"

St. Mary's Academy orchestra performed. It was somewhat unbalanced, having two pianos, five violins, a mandolin, and four sweet potatoes or ocarinas. They did "The Flight of the Bumblebee," but it sounded more like a traveling wasp. Two girls sang "Trees." Another one did an aria from *La Traviata.* We had punch and salmon sandwiches, Father Hady assuring all who were fasting for Lent to pitch in because they were excused for such a memorable event.

After the meal we moved around a bit but the trouble was that the parents kept on sitting there and staring at us. A tiny girl called Virginia asked me if I would meet her on Sunday at the bandstand in the park because she wanted to run away. I swallowed her story and went around with my heart pumping madly until I saw her later pointing me out to a group of other girls and laughing madly.

Then a guest speaker appeared. He was lean and cadaverous, and looked like a telephone pole with a mustache. He had a pair of spectacles (with a black ribbon mysteriously attached) that kept slipping off his nose. Mother St. John sat on one side of him and Father Hady on the other. They whispered among themselves and finally Father Hady stood up, fidgeted with his collar, and said, "Dr. Harold M. O'Leary is a prominent specialist and he has something to say which should be of special use at this time of year to boys and girls."

Dr. O'Leary nodded and moved his body around as if he wanted to include everybody in the auditorium.

"I am the father of fourteen boys and girls and my wife is here. Stand up, dear."

A frail little woman inched up the wall from her seat on the side lines and abruptly dropped back in her chair, seemingly exhausted.

"See what I mean," whispered Bill Zinger, "it's going to be a sex orgy."

Dr. O'Leary grasped the edges of the table and leaned forward saying, "Man is a creature put on this earth to serve God in as high a way as possible. Young people have a deep responsibility to keep intact the glorious gifts they have been endowed with, so that when they come into their lifely estate, they do so unashamed of anything. The temples of our bodies are holy, for they are the earthly repositories of our souls. It is a wonderful thing in later life for a man and a woman to be graced with God's blessing, as we have been. . . ." He nodded to his fragile wife, who tried to stand up again but couldn't quite make it.

"I thank God for keeping me through those days of temptation that my life might be filled to the full with the joyousness of existence within the comforting cadence of God's blessings."

It went on and on—and on—and we marched home silently. As

we were going to bed Michael Callahan made a remark that must still be treasured at St. Gerald's.

"As for me, I would just as soon run the risk of getting sick on more saltpeter or even going to hell for abusing myself than take a chance on another thing like that."

Chapter 12

SABOTAGE

———◆———

Lent was a testing time. It was a season for penance. Most of us felt that the regime was penitential at the best of times, but the fathers had the idea that true mortification was what we needed.

"This is a time for all of us to give up luxuries," thundered the disciplinarian; "we must make amends for sinful lapses in our lives. It is a time to develop true joy in our souls. It is the heavenly joy that the early martyrs enjoyed while on earth."

The rumor started. Someone was going to be made an ultimate example and be burned at the stake. The disciplinarian had the eyesight of a primitive and the hearing of a cannibal on the trail of a fat missionary. He heard the whisper.

"Otto, what were you saying?"

"I was thinking of giving up steak for Lent, Father."

"Steak, eh. A worthy sacrifice! But where would you get . . ." he stopped and then thundered, "don't be facetious. Be quiet. Sit down, Alberts, and don't act stupid."

He had been caught out. Steak had never appeared on our menu. The animals may have had such a cut on their carcasses but we never saw it. It was rumored that steaks had once been ordered for a visit by the head of the order but the staff were so inexperienced in such things that they had boiled them, and steaks were never purchased again.

"Come on, now, boys, let's not make jokes like our diminutive friend here."

Otto was furious. He didn't mind being called "little" or "small," but he thought "diminutive" was somehow obscene. He had set the tone, and another student suggested giving up "fresh fish." There was an angry rumbling in the hall. I had heard from senior students how the quality of the fish was of an even lower order than usual during the Lenten regimen of abstinence.

"And go on iron rations," snapped the irate priest, whose sharp features were wrinkling into anger. "I have a suggestion. I propose we give up the luxury of butter."

Since he was in charge of purchases for the college, there was a note of warning in his voice. He may have been thinking of personal sacrifice for Lent. We thought of him as seeing chances for further economies in the budget.

"Dismissed."

Having tossed out the bomb, he then let us out of the study hall fifteen minutes early.

"He's going to do it," said Otto, streaking for a vacant room and a newly discovered listening post.

We went straggling back to the dormitory. Up to this point, the butter, a far cry from the product of my mother's churning on the farm, had been semi-rancid, but tolerated. Now it assumed tremendous importance.

"He wouldn't do it."

"Oh, yes, he would, and he will."

"A person will never be able to eat that bread without butter. It'll stick in your throat."

We told the prefect of the dormitory that Otto had been called to straighten books in the library and we went to bed. An hour later, Otto sneaked into his bed.

"I was stuck," he said, "the rector and the sergeant-major had an argument in the next room and I couldn't get out. He says it will be a valuable penance, but the rector is not sure it's a good idea."

The rector had every desire to see the students do individual penance in Lent but he was afraid that students might write home and say butter had been cut off as an enforced discipline.

"The disciplinarian won," admitted Otto, "because he said we wasted a lot of butter and this would be a valuable experience for all of us."

It was a valuable experience. For the first time in my life, I discovered the difficulties of organizing resistance. The older boys set up battle plans. It was a mass confusion at first and would have failed except for the fact that the prefect, a young seminarian, had already run afoul of the disciplinarian. In addition, he was a country boy who didn't appreciate reductions in food.

There was no butter at breakfast and only the disciplinarian sat at the staff table. He ignored the table thumping. The back of the group's first resolve to go on hunger strike broke because we were all hungry and pitched in to eat.

"How about a delegation?"

The proposal came at the end of a squabbling, noisy conference in the gymnasium at recess time. There was no butter at noon. At four-thirty a group went to meet the rector. They were belligerent and angered him.

"I was prepared to rescind the whole idea," he said with some heat, "but your tone is self-defeating, and now I don't think it will be a bad thing if you make the sacrifice."

For a week we had no butter. We had partial hunger strikes, an attempt to have mass sickness, and an accumulation of actions that all failed abysmally because of disorganization. Then I learned the power of the press. Johnny King knew a reporter on the New Gordon *Record*, and we planted a story to the effect that St. Gerald's College was going broke and had had to discontinue serving butter as an economy measure.

Butter was reinstated at the next meal. In spite of any number of inquisitions and test trials no one squealed on Johnny. He was a hero; thereafter we tended to glorify the power of the press.

But Lenten discipline pervaded the place. It began each day

when we awakened to a bell in the dim early morning and moved much like automatons to a prescribed schedule. The bell had a snarly and miserable sound. It tore into your dreams, bringing the ugly reality of the daily grind. From bell time on, we were pushed, urged, and cajoled from chapel to dining room to classroom and even into recreation. We had the same kind of kinship as convicts because the high red fence surrounding the campus was as bad as an unscalable stone wall. When night came, we had the final indignity of having a light blink at us as if by so doing it could automatically bring sleep with the blankness of the darkened dormitory surrounding.

The days ground slowly on. Something had to give. Somebody had to crack. We waited. When it happened it concerned Tony and Jerry. They had a mutual interest—girls. They spent all their waking hours planning how to escape college discipline. They had plenty of money and it was assumed that some went to bribe the cleaning staff to protect escape routes. Then there was a crisis. Before the morning bell, a rumor spread that the disciplinarian had found someone AWOL.

"It's Tony."

This was the rumor. Tony, however, appeared in chapel. It became a game to try to determine who was missing.

"It's Jerry," whispered Otto.

Sure enough, there was no sign of the curly-haired blond lad from Quebec. At breakfast the dining room seethed with excitement. We were kept for ten minutes after the meal while a white-faced priest read Scriptures. No one heard him. Something was up. We heard a car on the cindered courtyard. Something was being dragged down the stairs from the private rooms.

"He's dead and that's the body," whispered Johnny King.

The rector walked in. The priest stopped reading.

"Mr. Jerry Lacombe is no longer a student at St. Gerald's. There are rules and regulations in this college made for your protection. They are part of the discipline and our educational system. As I told you before, those who violate those rules must leave. If anyone doesn't agree with our decision, they, too, are free to leave."

We were dismissed. A pall lay over the college. Jerry was gone, and students discovered affection they never knew they had for him.

"Just listen to the blather," said Little Otto. "They're a gang of hypocrites who didn't even rate a nod from him. I thought he was a snob. He was practically asking to get kicked out."

Then Tony spread the word that "Baldy," an uncommunicative janitor, had ratted on Jerry. Up to this point, he had been accepting money for letting Jerry or Tony out a furnace room door and giving them a key, which they deposited inside when they returned. The rumor stirred us to plan dire things for the squat, shaven-headed Polish immigrant who smelled of garlic and onions. Someone suggested a "kangaroo court" and we agreed, although most of us didn't know what it was.

We were all somewhat frightened. The idea of expulsion from college had a dire ring to it. I could imagine the repercussions in my home. I was not on intimate terms with Tony, but when he borrowed some notes I decided to ask his reaction.

"Oh, there's not so much to being expelled. I was kicked out in Barcelona, Paris, and Geneva before I came here. Still, it would be a bad thing if it happened here. My family told me they will not send me to any more colleges. I have to go to work then, and this I do not like. I will be good."

That wasn't very comforting. Then the impression spread that Jerry had wanted to get expelled, and the matter of "Baldy," the informer, died down. Nothing might have happened if it hadn't been for the incident at the Tuck Shop.

Johnny King, on a Saturday noon, was a sartorial display. He had a new gray suit with notched lapels and bell-bottom pants, because, he had informed us, he was meeting a redhead from the soda fountain. It must have moved him to rash confidence because as Baldy walked through the cramped quarters of the Tuck Shop, Johnny said, "Still telling tales to the priests, eh?"

The caretaker, black and grimy from a session with the aged

furnace, clamped his hands on Johnny's shoulders. It became a fracas. The suit was grease-marked, Johnny lost his free period, and the disciplinarian was inclined to accept Baldy's story.

"It doesn't make sense that Mr. Waszilewski would attack a student in an unpremeditated fashion. There must have been some provocation. I have been annoyed for some time at the way students treat people like Peter. The incident is closed."

It wasn't, however. Peter Waszilewski, through Michael Callahan (who was Polish on his mother's side), appeared to want to make amends. Michael explained to King that the janitor was sorry and would have the suit cleaned. We urged Johnny at least to take advantage of the offer.

Three days later, Johnny was prancing around the dormitory screaming and crying.

"Look what the slob did to my suit. Just look. It's ruined."

The suit was clean. In fact, it was faded and it had shrunk to the point where it might fit Otto. King went to the basement with fire in his eyes.

"Ja—clean."

Baldy couldn't understand what all the fuss was about. His wife had cleaned the suit. There wasn't a trace of grease on it.

"Ja—clean."

King looked as if he were going to explode in anger. Someone brought Callahan down. He listened incredulously, it seemed, to a torrent of Polish from Waszilewski. Then he started to laugh, finally sitting on the floor holding his sides.

"She—she—Mrs. Peter—she—" he stammered out, finally, "wanted to do the best job possible, so she boiled the suit."

Nothing would convince Johnny King the janitor was not a fiend. He conceived that Peter Waszilewski would in turn get all of us by one trick or another. He started wailing about Jerry. Revenge had to be taken on behalf of Jerry. That's how we all managed, after lights out one night, to be in the darkened auditorium. We had been threatened with physical violence if we didn't appear. "You be there or else it won't be good for you."

There was a lot of fussing behind the curtains on stage. Loud whispers. Things falling, and then from a side door appeared a rectangle of light and Peter was standing there.

"Wat dis—wat you want?"

About twenty students fell on him and the noises were petrifying—especially because there was only the dim light from the door. After what seemed to be a dreadful struggle, the janitor was taken up on the stage by the side entrance. The curtain went up and in the light of candles there was a tableau to rival the Salem witch trials. The boys wore shroudlike affairs over their heads.

"Peter Waszilewski, you have been charged by this assembled court of your peers as being . . ."

We knew it was Aleck McCaffrey, in spite of his disguised voice. He faltered on the charge. Johnny King supplied the words.

"You are responsible for lying to the dean and cheating the students."

Peter gave some signs of struggling and several boys leaped at him, upsetting the candles.

"Dam' fools—dam' fools—tell the fadda. Get you sons of bitches. Kill you. Kill you!"

The accused was shouting so loudly we began to worry. During the half-hour or so after lights out, we were usually safe because the prefects and disciplinarians used to stay in the billiard room and drink coffee. Although the auditorium was in the lower part of the gymnasium building apart from the main building, this noise might rouse them.

"Let's get out," whispered Otto.

Order was re-established on the stage. Michael Callahan spoke in Polish. There was a long conversation and finally he turned and said, "Sorry, fellows, but Peter tells me Jerry told him to tell the dean. His father wouldn't let him quit because he was afraid he would get married."

Waszilewski broke out in a fresh torrent of words. This time Michael roared with laughter. It took some time to calm him down. Finally, with the tears streaming from his face, he said,

"And guess who he's marrying! The redhead at the soda fountain, and she's Peter's daughter."

"Ja," grinned Peter, "nice girl. Jerry fine man. Gots lots of dollars."

Then a voice cut through the half light.

"What are you boys doing?"

The lights came on full. Here was most of the student body in bathrobes and slippers and a weird assortment of masked figures on stage. The questioner was one of the younger priests, who had only left St. Gerald's as a graduate a few years before.

"Well, what's the explanation?"

Then Otto spoke up. "We're learning Polish, Father."

It looked momentarily as if the priest were going to explode. Then he reached over and pulled off the master switch. I think he wanted to disguise his own laughing.

"If you managed to get in without lights, I guess you can get out. Now remember, no noise. I'm going to be in the front corridor saying my office and I don't want to be disturbed."

We understood. In return, he was accorded the co-operation of all students in the study hall or in his classroom. The same could not be said for many of the other instructors. As the pressure of Lenten obligations became harder, a sabotage movement became apparent.

It was bitter cold. Dormitories and gymnasium were drafty and chilly. The study hall was overheated, and since it was in the same building as the offices and studies of the priests and lay teachers, they were used to heat. But for us the seven-to-nine period of study each night was suffocating, and Father Hady, who had a dread fear of catching cold, wouldn't let us open a window.

When you are bored and captive, odd things distract. Gas produced by the strange assortment of cheap foods, from cabbage to beans, fascinated us. Ordinarily circumspect boys took pride in their ability to produce explosive, discordant, or semi-musical sounds.

Jimmy Auden took a particular delight in waiting until the

dormitory was quiet, pulling back the covers, and shattering the silence. The prefect was wise. He flicked the lights on without getting out of bed. He left them on for a minute. They went out and we strained for anti-climactic effects. Three or four minutes later the lights would come on again and that would put a damper on our activity.

Finally someone developed the Great Gas conspiracy to get our own back on Hady for pressure-cooking us in the study hall. We had been in the habit of working the gas off during the time between supper and the seven o'clock study period.

"Don't waste them. Hang on to everything you've got. Save your ammunition no matter what happens. But when you're in that room give everything you've got in you. Concentrate. We'll gas old Hady out of the place."

Those were the orders. We concentrated. We moved as little as possible before study period. We settled in and concentrated on the task. There were several painful episodes of lack of self-control on the part of one or two enthusiasts, but they did contribute to the general rankness.

By seven-thirty the heat, the smell of steaming clothes, and the fetid odor were overpowering. By the third night several boys became sick and were excused, but Father Hady would not allow the windows to be opened.

"No, no. It is nice and comfortable. Just right, and we don't want to catch colds."

He beamed. He actually seemed to be enjoying it. We were straining and smothering, and he was actually appearing to be enjoying it. It was a puzzle. We could hardly stand ourselves and rushed outside at nine to take deep breaths of fresh, cold air before being herded into the chapel.

"Look," said Otto on the fifth night, "it won't work. That holy crow is actually adding to it. He's just like my mother. I can tell from his face. Father will let go anytime but Mother smothers hers. She walks and lets little ones go. That's what he's doing. When he walks up and down like that with that funny smile on his face he's dropping them all over the place. The only thing is, he *likes* them."

The conspiracy ended; we stopped saving our ammunition for the study hall and suffered the heat.

Chapter 13

RETREAT

———◆———

It began so simply—them or us! Yet as the days and months passed by we began to realize that something had changed. We were linked, priests and boys verging on manhood, in a form of lock step.

Throughout the school there was an overwhelming conscious-ness of sin, confession, absolution, and Communion. For some it was euphoric. For others it produced a gnawing, inner sense of puzzlement.

"Per Christum Dominum nostrum Jesum Christum qui vivit et regnat per omnia saecula saeculorum."

The votive lights flickered in the chapel. We left it in the soft, spring nights and went back to our rooms or dormitories, and there was a strange silence. The nights were sensuous. Here and there a boy mumbled prayers as if building defenses.

I dreamed of places other than Clover. I knew that the world held something more than St. Gerald's College. The hungers and desires of adolescence crowded in on me. Somehow the words "Gain the whole world and lose your immortal soul" no longer inspired the same awesome fear.

I became fascinated with speculating about the priests. I sup-pose we all wondered what had made them that way. Many were normally cheerful. Divested of their soutanes and collars, they laughed about the same things as we did, enjoyed nature, and perhaps even cried.

Professionally, it was a different matter. "It's them or us," sounded the call of the more recalcitrant students. Yet, I wondered. The problem was caused by my realizing that they were human beings. They had the same jealousies and rivalries as anyone else. We knew that Father Bohmer sometimes drank too much. The rector, relieving him on one occasion of a class, said, in a rare moment of compassion, that Father Bohmer had suffered in the 1914–18 war.

The kindest of all the priests was Father Polly. In later years, when I saw the apologetic figure, bald head, and the kewpie-doll wrinkled face of the actor Donald Meek, he seemed the living incarnation of Father Polly. He was a misfit. He didn't subscribe to the rector's theory of cool, perfect management. He had lost a parish because he insisted on dipping into the finances to pay relief for poor parishioners.

At confession time there were four priests each located in the living-room office of their two-room suites on the way to the chapel. The line-up in front of Father Polly's confessional would stretch all the way back into the study hall. The other priests had the odd straggler or one or two boys without fear. When the rector walked down the corridor with his hands bulked under his robe, his face was unhappy and frowning.

"Straighten up there and don't lounge!" He might also mutter something under his breath about the other priests wasting valuable time. Yet he never dared order us to another confessor. That was an unwritten rule; you could go to the confessor of your choice. Our choice was Father Polly. And it worked very well, because he seldom taught in a classroom.

There was one handicap. The old priest was slightly deaf. Mindful of the line-up outside you had to try to speak just loud enough for him to hear. If you mumbled and he caught only a fragment of a sentence, he would repeat it, and like all deaf people with no idea of volume, he might bring it out in a whisper or a roar.

"Had bad thoughts? Thinking about girls?"

Those were the times you crept out of the confessional and melted into a dark corner of the chapel. But Father Polly was a gentle man. He was understanding of our problems of vocation. "My boy, don't be discouraged. Don't be pushed into thinking you have to be a priest or religious. Remember, the world doesn't smell and feel like this place. It is a very bad idea to get all worked up here and feel that you have heard the whisper of God in your ear. It may only be the rector's breath." He smiled then, and it didn't seem possible to us that a teacher could be so gentle and kind.

Then we faced the retreat. The retreat was for massaging our spiritual lives. We had several shorter ones, but the principal one was to prepare for the trip home at Easter. It lasted from Wednesday morning to Sunday night and was marked by silence at all times and perpetual adoration to the exposed Blessed Eucharist in the chapel.

The retreat broke down the last defenses of many students. Up to this point they resisted holy pressure. They treasured their resistance to holy control and dreamed about having enough nerve to sneak out at nights, date girls, and, in general, have at least a decent chance at hell-raising.

They didn't take the impact of the retreat into account. We shuffled into chapel on Wednesday morning and spent the day in finding ways of breaking the silence rule. Notes were exchanged and code signals were used—somehow, it was impossible to pass another student without at least trying to communicate.

"Boyle, were you talking?"

"No, Father."

"Well, what were you doing?"

"Communicating with Finegan."

"How?"

"A note about trigonometry."

"Very well, but remember silence is not being imposed here as an idle fancy. It is very important for you in these days ahead to avoid distractions."

Perpetual adoration was maintained by always having four students in the chapel where the Blessed Sacrament was exposed on the altar in the monstrance. Every half-hour two of the students would be replaced. I can still feel the prefect's hand on my shoulder. "Come on, get up and carry your shoes. Don't make any more noise than possible."

It was the middle of the night. The only light in the room came from the street lamps, four stories below, and the normal glow of the city. You went to the washroom and dressed in a sleepy, numbed way.

"You fellows have five minutes to get to chapel."

It was cold in the courtyard in the morning. The city was quiet, and the old buildings seemed to be resting. As we walked down the corridor past the teachers' suites, we could imagine them comfortable, while we faced an hour of trying to stay awake on the hard pews of the chapel. The priest inside the chapel door looked up from where he was kneeling on the *prie-dieu*, checked his list, and nodded for us to relieve two of the boys draped from seats to kneelers. Thus began another daily vigil. The chapel had only the ruby sanctuary lamp, a dim light by a statue, and candles burning on the side altar. It was chilly because the central heating system was always turned down at night. It was spring and there was the excuse that lack of heat kept the boys from sleeping.

We started with bolt-upright attention, somewhat dismayed by the sight of the two remaining boys slouched into sleeping positions. The priest glided by on soft feet and poked them into wakefulness. He came by and whispered: "Say your prayers . . ." adding as an afterthought, "It will keep you awake. And remember, there are detentions for going to sleep."

Chilled and half asleep and with hunger pangs pinching our stomachs, we hallucinated into various forms of ecstasy.

"Oh, please, God, help me to be good . . . grant me the privilege of a vocation. I want to serve . . ."

The advantages of being a religious came swimming into our minds. It seemed possible to transcend the gray world of St. Gerald's College and become ordained. The silence and the night! I imagined ordination and saying my first Mass and looking down at my mother and father and seeing the tears in their eyes and then . . .

"Boyle, wake up . . . you're a disgrace, sleeping like that."

It was my relief. Yet the experience made an impression, and as the days of the retreat wore on there was less and less respect for the smart ones who tried to break the rules.

"I am delighted," said the rector, making an exception and allowing us the privilege of talking at the Friday noon meal, "that so many of you boys are making visits to the chapel during your free periods. This is a good sign and you are to be congratulated."

The talk period swelled at first into a froth of conversation and then slackened off. In spite of everything, we didn't want to break the spell. There were a few who didn't share our enthusiasm, and they spent their time in the gymnasium, noisily exercising; but we were impaled by the emotion of the moment.

The retreat closed on a triumphant note of Benediction in the chapel. There is no exercise of the Church more calculated to give you a lift than Benediction . . . the chanting of the Te Deum . . . the incense and the raising of the Host. We went off silently to our beds, somehow certain that if God hadn't at least spoken to us, if we listened hard enough and long enough, we might have heard a whisper.

During the next few days many of us composed letters to our parents, hoping to give them some encouragement in their daily battle in the world of trial and temptation. These missives were often filled with superficial explanations of religious feelings that were destined to be a continuing source of embarrassment later on. Mothers responded with letters so filled with thankfulness that we could imagine them as tearstained.

But the effect of the retreat was soon erased in the daily routine of work and life at school. Our true natures began to come out from under the anesthesia, and we began to doubt about applying to the bishop for a bursary as a priest. Then a new tactic became apparent. Vocation days were held. Free periods were invaded by special speakers. Most were graduates of St. Gerald's. They were of all types and kinds, but they were all priests.

"Now, fellows, you have to get in there and pitch on the Lord's team. That devil is a hard one to beat, but you can do it."

That was the athletic type. He invariably dropped in to the locker room. All he managed to do was make the boys angry. But we also faced the confidential type. "It may be a little difficult," he said to me in a library session, "but you must try. Now, I want to tell you—how a vocation came to me—"

Michael Callahan, a cynic, said it was all caused by the rector.

"He wants scalps. There's the odd one like that. Wants to hand a lot of vocations to the bishop. But he's not making out very well. He'll crack. He was watching us through the door and he could see we weren't paying much attention. He'll try something new."

Then there was a warm night when the heat had somehow got turned on by mistake, and everybody was restless. As I flipped my pillow to try and get a cool side I became aware of someone standing in the aisle in front of my cot. It was Father Hady.

"What's the matter with you?"

"Can't sleep."

"Ho—ho—something bothering you?"

He moved in beside my cot.

"Not sleeping. My boy, you know the consequence of bad thoughts."

The only bad thoughts I had at that moment were angry ones about him.

"Did you hear me?"

Then he became aware of other heads popping up from blankets.

"So we have a problem, have we?"

Then he strode to the wall box outside the prefect's door and
roared at us.

"Bad thoughts are the enemy of good Christians. Into the
showers—all of you—make them cold." Of course, four of the
smarter, older boys ended up the next day with "fake" symptoms
of cold or pneumonia or something. The school buzzed. The boys
in the private rooms screamed "Water Babies!" at every opportunity. The teachers looked ashamed. The rector was quiet. The
inspirational speakers stopped coming, but the bishop made a
surprise visit. He was a friendly giant of a man who smoked long,
black cigars, and he moved the disciplinarian to another school.

We were deposited in the steamy, sensuous April of that Easter
in our respective homes. Seeding was in full swing. The entire
valley was geared to it. But my family had moved from the farm
just before Christmas and now ran a general store.

Something had changed. I was later to realize that Father
moved at exactly the wrong time. The depression was tightening.
Farmers without cash were trying to barter for necessities, and
Father, like any other storekeeper with suppliers' bills to pay,
needed hard cash.

There was tension for the first time. Money, which was scarcely
mentioned while we were farmers, except at tax time, now became
a preoccupation. Commercial travelers waited for long periods
in the store before finally confessing, "If you could only give me
an order, no matter how small, it would help. The boss would at
least know I tried."

Men I had known for all my life as confident and resolute
would wait for my father, rather than speak to me. In the whispered conversation there was a note of desperation, or even of
pleading. They simply wanted credit. Later, looking over the files
in the old cabinet, I found that they were already in debt.

The store was a fabulous place of counters, shelves, barrels,
boxes, and crates. The stock ranged from a barrel of salted her-
rings to bolts of gingham. Crumbling cheese that bit your tongue
came in enormous waxed blocks that had to be cut in layers with

a stout, waxed cord. While my father operated a whirling appara-
tus that tested cream, I candled eggs before a hole cut in a stove-
pipe fitted over a gasoline lamp.

Where I had once been attracted to listening to the stories of
the men, I now had a reawakened urge to write. Hour by hour
during the Easter holiday afternoons I scribbled in an exercise
book. There were few customers because they were working on
the land, and my former classmates were distant. They listened
politely when I talked about college and when I finished they went
back to local gossip. I wrote from an inner solitude. Luckily my
family seemed to think that my writing had some connection with
work at college.

There was another awkward session with Father Morrison
about becoming a priest. I had served Mass, uncomfortably aware
that my clearly recited Latin responses betrayed my college training and contrasted with the old priest's. He simply said the first
word or two, "*Per Christum*" and buzzed the rest out in a hum.

At Communion time, I dropped the gold paten and the Host
slipped from the priest's trembling fingers. Then I did the un-
forgivable thing of ducking to retrieve it. Our heads collided
solidly, so that Mass ended groggily for both of us.

I had a vague sense of sin because the paten had dropped from
my fingers when Mrs. Lindley leaned forward and her blouse
gaped. I was unprepared for what had been disclosed of her buxom
charms and suspected that it may have also unnerved the pastor.

In the vestry he slowly removed his vestments. There was a certain significance in his holding onto the chasuble. I remembered
the prayer to be said, "Gird me, O Lord, with the cincture of
purity and extinguish in my heart the fire of concupiscence."

"I suppose you have given up all thoughts of being a priest."

"Well—no—in a way."

He put away the vestments and slid the drawer in, seemingly
disposing of the matter.

"Beware of temptation. The fires of hell are hot."

That flared in my mind. Then, at the Easter dance in the township hall, Mrs. Lindley selected me for a fox trot, smothered me in the hollow of her bosom and dragged me around the floor for what seemed an eternity.

That night my fantasies were more vivid than usual. All growing boys have dreams and fantasies. Mine were natural and yet in a way different.

Chapter 14

EASTER MUSIC

———————◆———————

I was caught between two worlds. St. Gerald's College was a threshold to many things I had never been conscious of before. Art was a magical thing that could suspend you in an inner tension that was near physical. The dimensions of strange, distorted forms and the interplay of colors induced in me feelings that ranged from joy to the edge of sorrow.

The lushness of skin tones of angels, cherubim, and plump women aroused me. There was the voluptuous mystery of colors in books of prints a forgotten member of the order had brought back from Rome. They were neglected in the library. Wisely, I never mentioned the nudes to the librarian, an ascetic man who constantly warned against the temptations of the flesh, as if he were scourging a private devil.

It was so different from the calendars and prints that up to this point had satisfied my senses at home. They served a purpose in our house. They broke the monotony of bare walls.

But there was more than this. I had accepted the country without question. Now, I felt as if I were on a quest of some kind. There were earth smells in the swamp and the lushness of willows and trees misting into buds and unfolding into leaves.

The valley hummed with sounds. Men were busy on the land. The air buzzed with insects. Life was pulsing and I wanted to revel in it. It was rich and rewarding simply to be on a hillside in the sun, warm and lost in contemplation of the clouds.

This was my home. My people had come from the harshness of famine and persecution to a wilderness of trees. They cleared the land and on the farm so lately vacated, their first log house still stood. I had gone into it countless times to feed the hens or gather warm eggs that nestled beside a polished white stone or a porcelain doorknob, supposed to induce laying by the power of suggestion.

This had once been the land of the Huron Indians. Earlier I had imagined them and the Iroquois as the cruel torturers of such Canadian martyrs as Jean de Brébeuf.

They were closer now. In fantasy, I could see their cooking fires. Their women were real. If I listened closely, the cries of the children at play and the sounds of the dogs yelping and quarreling would drown out the sounds of a farm community at spring seeding.

At Clover, a man had put up a two-story house, sold whisky and meals, and rented space for travelers and horses. Another man placed a dam across the Maitland River and used the force of the pent-up water to drive the wheel that turned the stones that ground the settlers' corn and grain. It was a crossroads and they prospered and in time the Indians vanished.

They were transients in my childhood who came in the spring to camp by the river flats. Their tents were dowdy canvas affairs. The lodgepoles and painted hide coverings were gone. They wore ill-fitting white man's clothing and drove battered Model T cars. Their women still cooked over open fires but used dented, blackened pots and pans. The men trapped muskrats, much to the annoyance of locals who did the same. In the fall, the Indians came back to pick flax and dig ginseng root.

Thinking of them made me sad. They were silent people who suffered some harassment with dignity. Only my father seemed to know and respect their silences, and they trusted him. But, at this Easter, thinking of them made me want to cry.

I realized for the first time that I was part of a process. We had come so recently from pioneer rawness. The iron kettle my great-grandmother used to cook with over the open fire in the fireplace was a receptacle for watering cattle in our farm barnyard.

The things I grew up with were neglected at the farm. At the store, gasoline lamps had replaced the kerosene ones of the farm. My father dreamed of harnessing the power of a windmill or using batteries to generate electricity to light the store and house. At school and college I used electricity without thinking about it.

To write came naturally as an outlet. I had to put down on paper this mystification about the conflicts. At first there were cumbersome odes to Indians. There was a fury somehow to make up for the indignities suffered by them at the hands of the whites.

"You really must be taking college seriously," observed my father.

Wisely, I didn't make any comment. The distance between writing was even more difficult to explain than that between Botticelli and a binder-twine calendar showing geese in flight from a pond under a threatening sky. My mother was puzzled but philosphical about the writing.

"It's something I don't understand, but I suppose you'll get it out of your system," she said, while tidying around where I was working at the table. "I suppose priests who become really good speakers must write a lot."

"It helps me with grammar and literature, Ma."

She nodded.

"I suppose. At least you're not chasing around after girls all the time. That's one good thing."

If the days of that Easter recess were filled with dreaming and writing, the nights were fevered and confused. The aching for a firmer grasp on the immediate history of my people was mild compared to the torment of physical longing. It was as if the confined and controlled time of college residence had left me vulnerable to every jiggle, bounce, and movement of female flesh.

My dreams were tormented and the cause of Indians and

settlers was forgotten as I turned to write about love. Here my ignorance was colossal. I knew at least something about Indians and ancestors. The ways of the flesh were wrapped in the harsh "don'ts" of catechism. It was never explicit. The whole matter was dangerous, and you were expected not to do what was never explained.

It had something to do with the urge to be with girls I had started to experience painfully at high school. It was my good or bad fortune to encounter only girls endowed with as much ignorance as myself. The fumblings were awkward. The main difficulty was identifying them as bad enough to be confessed. Trying it once or twice I had been caught by the extreme embarrassment of the confessor, who was trying to identify the gravity of the situation by use of indirect, discreet questions.

By the Thursday before I was to return to college, I burned by night and flamed by day. Every page of what I considered to be passionate outbursts had to be concealed in case any of the family might come upon them.

This Easter season of awakening induced emotions that ranged from despairing sadness to pure joy. I had scarcely been aware before of wind, rain, silence, or even the feel of the house when I came awake in the middle of the night. It held my family, but it was crammed with the presence of my grandmother, who died as quietly as she lived, in the great wooden bed with the spool-designed corner posts. My grandfather slept there now, alone.

I wanted to cry for him. I didn't know why. Creeping down the stairs, avoiding the boards that creaked, I went out to the night. It was pitch black. The country was still.

I was alone in the valley. That dim outline down the road was the fortresslike home of Jack Macdonald. Old Jack, who ruled his family like a laird, making them all bend to his will and go night and morning to the Continuing Presbyterian Church on Sundays. His small pinched wife had given up living and died over a washtub. His oldest boy had come back from the war in 1918, coughing up bits of his gassed lungs. His youngest son had defied him and married a Catholic. Now he went alone on Sundays, a proud hard man who refused to recognize all change just as he refused to believe in Church Union.

There were the Dolans in their small house. Mike and his wife and brood of seven children, who arrived at Clover station direct from Connemara.

"That was it, my lad. I had a five-pound note that a sharper convinced me was worth only five dollars and all of our belongings in a tin trunk and four cloth satchels."

Mike now owned his own farm and was the happiest man in the valley. And Red Sandy on the concession, with a nagging, redheaded mountain of a wife, who owned only debts but played the fiddle at every dance and loved whisky.

Perhaps that night I knew something I didn't know before. I like to think I did know that no matter where I went or what I did that these people would walk in my consciousness. But I would not stay here. The sense of having to move on had come from somewhere. I didn't know where. I knew it existed in me.

From somewhere, words I had tried to memorize at the instigation of a teacher flew back into my head like returning birds to a nest.

> "Creation sleeps! 'Tis as the general pulse
> Of life stood still, and Nature made a pause,—
> An awful pause! prophetic of her end."

The air hadn't changed but I was cold. In bed, my mind trembled with the discovery of meaning of so many things I had learned at high school and college as a discipline, without understanding. Sleep came with exhaustion. In the morning I had a hangover of troubled emotions.

"Mother, did you study poetry at school?"

Her hands and arms were floured as she stood at the kitchen table rolling out baking dough.

"Oh, you mean memory work."

She paused, trying to recall lines.

"Oh, yes. Let me see. There was one. 'Daffodils.' Now, how did it go? Hmm,

> *'I wandered lonely as a cloud*
> *That floats on high o'er hills'*—no—*'vales and hills,*
> *When all at once I saw a crowd,*
> *A host, of golden daffodils;*
> *Beside the lake, beneath the trees,*
> *Fluttering and dancing in the breeze.'*

"I liked that. I could never remember the rest of it. It was pretty. I think of it in the spring. . . . I think your father wants you to help in the store."

Just reciting the poetry had embarrassed her. I went into the store where my father was putting price tags on merchandise. I didn't ask him about poetry. I spent the day waiting on occasional customers and putting up five- and ten-pound bags of sugar from a barrel under the counter.

At night when the store was closed he sat down in the chair behind the overall counter where he kept accounts in a small desk.

"Got any idea of what you plan to do?"

"How do you mean?"

He scratched his head as if trying to help articulate a difficult question.

"Well, you know what your mother wants and—"

The conversation was as difficult as our attempts to communicate about sex. There were stops and starts and we circled the subject as if each of us were afraid to bring it out in the open. The ending was particularly unsatisfactory.

"I know that scribbling isn't going to get you anywhere. That stuff about the Indian girl and the lumberjack is—well, I hope your mother doesn't come on it."

My rage made me shake but no words came. All I could do was walk out the front door, slamming it after me. The road was quiet. There were no clouds. A new moon was a sliver of silver light. I walked until my anger ebbed. When I came back my grandfather

was sitting alone in the kitchen smoking his pipe. I could see the
coal of it glowing in the darkness and smell the pungent smoke.

"Been walking?"

"Yeah. Are the folks in bed?"

"Tomorrow's Saturday and they have to be up early. Your dad
wants you to drive into Clover with the truck in the morning and
pick up some seed corn that was left there for him."

Usually there was a reluctance to let me drive the truck. It was
childish to be elated about such a thing but I was. I concealed it,
glad Grandfather couldn't see my face.

"Good."

"You'll be taking the train tomorrow night."

"Guess so."

"In case I don't get a chance, here's something for you."

In the darkness he passed me a bill. Upstairs, by the light of a
match, I identified it as ten dollars. That, with my muskrat-trapping
money, gave me twenty-seven dollars. I felt rich.

It was only a Tin Lizzie, a Model T roadster with the small
metal back replaced by a homemade box. It was my father's truck.
It skittered and bounced along the gravel road on the hard rubber
tires leaving a dust cloud. I was enthralled—like every boy of the
day—by cars.

There was a sensation of power. A pull of the gas lever on the
steering column could produce a surge of what felt like tremendous speed. It was a challenge to race across the river bridge and
try to go as far as possible up the hill before resorting to the pedal
that put it into low gear and a crawling pace.

A stalled motor meant pulling on the hand brake, quickly
putting stones behind the rear wheels, as the brake was never to
be trusted. Then there was a delicate adjustment of spark lever,
gas, and choke and a laborious cranking to bring the motor back
into coughing activity.

That April day was charmed. At Munro's Store the sacks of
father's seed corn were piled by the door. Mr. Munro, a lean,

solemn man who wore a straw boater and apron, summer and winter, treated me to a cream soda.

"Do me a favor, lad," he said, handing me a parcel. "You see that white house just the third from last up your road?"

I had noticed a white sign in front of the old McGarvey place. "Sure."

"Mrs. Marshall, the new hairdresser, wants this five pounds of linseed meal and my delivery boy has gone away down to the flats with some grocery orders and won't be back until noon. Could you drop it off for me?"

There was a neat sign hanging from a post in front of the white frame house. It said, "Edythe Marshall, Beauty Parlor."

I stopped and walked up the pathway fringed with red tulips. Before I could even touch the bell, the door opened. There was Mrs. Marshall.

"Oh, thank you."

Edythe Marshall was . . . to this day I can't really remember what she really looked like. She was blond and a vision that embraced all my senses of spring and growth and pleasure, and I stared.

"You're not Mr. Munro's regular boy."

I stammered out an explanation. Who I was and how I was delivering the parcel—and the words were coming from somewhere but I was staring. Mrs. Marshall blushed. That I noticed.

"Do you have time to come in for a cup of coffee?"

We passed the door to the front room, all white like a hospital with some strange devices set up around the wall. The second room was a lair of lacy curtains and chintz-covered chairs and an overpowering smell of scents. A fat gray cat looked at me insolently and closed its eyes as if dismissing my presence.

"You wait here and I'll get the coffee—"

Mrs. Marshall was trim in places and full in others and a great deal of the real woman showed. I had a startling view as she drained a glass with one arm held high. Her clothes were somehow misbuttoned or misconnected so that every movement disclosed varying patterns of skin of a texture which reminded me of my hidden treasure in the college library. While she was clattering dishes in the kitchen I sniffed her empty glass. I was naïve but I knew the smell of whisky.

"Mister—lad—how about a ginger ale? I haven't got any bloody coffee."

I would have settled for acid, hemlock, or bitters. She sat and sipped her drink and pulled on a cigarette. I sat and was conscious of my overalls, feet, arms, legs, ears, uncombed hair, and Mrs. Marshall. She was puffing furiously and apparently had forgotten about me. I tried looking at a picture on the wall but it was explicit about nudity and I looked back at Mrs. Marshall, now disclosing a great expanse of pink thighs.

"So you're the college boy, eh? I'll bet you have a hell of a time at college."

She winked. I was hot. The room was stuffy and the smell of perfume was making me dizzy.

"This is a stinking village. I don't know why I came here. Wanna know why I came here? I'll tell you why I came here. A man—a fella in this place—this hick town—set me up—well—not really— I mean he lived in Handrich and he wanted to see me—sometimes—you know how it is."

The wink was deliberately slow.

"Poor bastard died. Now I'm stuck here. A few women come to get hair done—facials—but they hate me. They just want to see the fast Edythe Marshall. Do you like me?"

She was tipsy and sitting in the chair by the door, which was my only exit.

"Oh yes, Mrs. Marshall, you're a very nice woman."

She laughed, upsetting her glass.

"Oh dear. Good rye wasted. You—would you like a drink?"

I was alternately fascinated and horrified. I could agree to a drink and while she was in the kitchen make a dash for the Model T. This was impractical. I had visions of rushing out only to find the car wouldn't go, or else breaking my arm if there was an over-load of spark while cranking. That was a Model T hazard.

Salvation came in the form of a customer. Mrs. Marshall stiffened, met the lady formally, installed her in the front room, and came back to where I cowered as if I were actually guilty of something.

"Look, I like you. I like talking to you. I'm lonely and you're a nice strong boy. God, you're really a man. Can you come back?"

Admission that I was going away that night didn't stop the blond beautician.

"You come back here by seven. The train doesn't go until ten. Please. I want to talk to you. You promise. I'm lonely. You come back and see Edythe."

My tongue failed and I nodded. Then she put her arms around my neck and I felt a woman's full passionate kiss for the first time. I stumbled out and somehow drove home. I unloaded the truck and went into the store.

There were several customers. My mother was showing someone dress goods. Father, weighing out nails, was squinting at the beam scales. My grandfather, coming up from the cellar carrying a coal-oil can, took a look at me and, grabbing me by the arm, hustled me to the kitchen.

"Here, take a look at yourself."

He pushed me into the washroom, where a mirror hung over the sink.

"Good God, where did you get that paint on your face? Where the hell were you?"

My mouth was ringed with red lipstick. When I grabbed for a towel, he stopped me.

"Get that on the towel and your mother will be in a real tizzy. Were you playing house with somebody? My God, and they think you're going to be a priest. Come on out in the shed and we'll find something to wipe it off with."

Natural caution kept me from telling him about Mrs. Marshall's invitation to go back and see her. The old man did one splendid thing. He didn't laugh at my story.

"She's a lonely woman, my boy. Loneliness drives people to odd things. People are cruel, too. Clover's no place for that business of hers. She should be in a bigger place. Hell, out here women don't fancy themselves up. They probably hate her, too. She's a pretty filly when she's dressed up."

He paused and looked directly at me. "Whether you were lucky or not to be interrupted—well"—he punched my shoulder— "suppose that depends on how you look at it. Just keep the whole thing to yourself."

The remainder of the day was a blurred affair. I schemed and tried to plan some way of getting a ride to the Clover station before seven o'clock. Nothing worked. That night I rode with my mother and father in the Model T.

"That's music I hear," exclaimed Father as we drove past the white house.

"That woman has one of those victrolas and Mrs. Eldred next door says she plays it real loud sometimes, so's they can hardly sleep."

"Sounds like nice music. I wish we had one."

"Hmph," answered Mother, "there are a lot of things we need a lot worse than a music machine."

It was a miserable train ride back to New Gordon.

Chapter 15

CHANGE

———————◆———————

Had I changed?

Something had happened to me during my first six months that went deeper than the mechanical scratching on my consciousness at high school. It is true that I was not really conscious of it; even now, the effects can only be tallied by what a priest probably meant when he said, "Think until your head hurts."

But thinking brought a boy to the end of a one-way street. There were no exits, no directions. If you wandered or strayed away from simple, almost fundamental issues, your teachers were baffled.

"If the Spanish were Catholics and they wanted to bring Christ to the New World, why did they kill so many people?"

The priest flushed.

"Ah, what have you been reading?"

He was a Canadian-raised son of German-farmer immigrants with a traditional mistrust of books. I was suspected because I worked in the library.

"Oh, nothing in particular, Father."

"Well, don't pay too much attention to those godless writers. The ways of the divine are mysterious and sometimes we are—we may find it strange to understand."

He was laboring for an answer and came up invariably with the same one.

"That's what faith is. We have faith to believe with. You must pray to keep it. Faith is not always easy to keep, so why don't you say an extra Rosary tonight."

The library was a refuge. Strangely enough, it was a library that had been accumulated with passion and a real love of books. But it was seldom used, probably because the regimen of teaching university students had made the process of learning deadly dull at what was originally intended to be an institution of higher learning. The teachers of a more philosophical bent moved to the novitiate.

Volume on volume of untouched books stood on the racks. Some were leather-bound. Others in German and Latin had red spines and a strange marbled form of binding. The inscriptions in spidery handwriting disclosed that many of them had been used in the early eighteen hundreds.

Science and mathematics were not my forte. Somehow, however, Johannes Kepler came into my consciousness. It was on a Saturday afternoon. The college was practically deserted and that day I hadn't enough money to go to a motion picture. I was supposed to dust a rack of never-used books. There was an end of note paper sticking up from one. It turned out to be a set of notes, yellowed but clear in that coppery-colored way of India ink that has aged. The penmanship was classical. A professor who wrote in English had obviously made random notes on a book by Kepler written in Latin. *Somnium* I knew to be dream.

"There is, of course, a world of doubt in this dream of being propelled into the atmosphere, dulled by opiates, and coming awake in a landing on the moon, and yet I am seized by the thought that unless man boldly plans such ventures, he will never accomplish anything."

There were other thoughts that I could not grasp, but some took hold.

"How do we know our scruples are any more valid than those of the men who opposed or ridiculed Columbus?"

The writer became a mystic at one point.

"I have often wondered if after death our souls are not whisked to another planet. Can the moon, that serene and lovely place of our imagination, be heaven? A paradise of vales and cool splendor! The fiery face of the sun may be the eternal burning of the place of lost souls."

Here was a new vision! I could hardly wait to show my treasure to someone. An elderly science teacher was on duty, in the absence of the bursar. When I found him he was dozing. He took the pages and looked them over.

"Hmmm. Yes. Probably Dietrich. He was here when I was a student. Became very queer indeed. They sent him to a parish because he was always stirring up trouble."

To my horror, he then proceeded to tear up the notes.

"Look, young man, if you want to stay working in that library, I advise you to work. You are there to keep it tidy, give out the books, and see that they are returned."

"But, Father—"

"No buts—just do as you should. Moon madness. That's what Dietrich had."

He roared with laughter.

"He got all worked up about people going to the moon. Just imagine! Going to the moon! Why don't you go to the movies and stop such nonsense."

An idea is not that easily killed. There was a strangely cynical lay teacher by the name of Donovan on the staff. An Irishman in the midst of the predominantly German order was a mystery in itself; Donovan was also reputed to have once been a Christian Brother and a brilliant teacher, who had suffered a breakdown.

I visited him in his two rooms, one a study and the other a bedroom. His teaching duties were light. He rarely left the campus and spent most of his time reading. He was fleshy, a constant cigarette smoker, and wore dark blue suits, white shirts, and black ties.

"Kepler. So you have fallen upon the celestial mathematician. An interesting case. Sit down, my boy."

He fished a book out of a shelf and then, without opening it, told me about the struggle of the lad born in 1571 to acquire an education while still working in his father's tavern.

"He wanted to be a Lutheran minister, managed to be educated in philosophy, but astronomy grabbed him. He was a professor of astronomy at Graz."

Donovan smiled.

"He was a persistent cuss. When there was a ban against Protestant teachers he went to Hungary. His wife was a Hungarian who was sick most of the time. He was always in debt. He was obsessed by the planets. The Jesuits actually saved his skin once or twice because I suppose they do value knowledge above petty bigotries of the moment. My God, what a life! When his first wife died, his three children were put down by something like a pox— smallpox—he moved to Linz in Austria, and that's where he published my favorite, *The Harmonies of the World*."

He moved to find another book.

"What prompts all this curiosity? Certainly not something you heard in one of our classrooms."

I mentioned Father Dietrich. His face turned white and then red, as if with anger. When the color subsided he sat in his chair.

"Poor old Dietrich. I just remember him. He was better in Latin than in English. Fascinating man, but he would start on something on a Saturday night and work through and forget to say Mass on Sunday. He had the idea that education was a process of involving students. So he would start on a thesis—and well— that's not orthodox. He had correspondence with a French priest who is a scientist—and a rather startling concept of God and creation—"

He stopped.

"Well, never mind. They—I should say the bishop and the head of the order—sent him off to some obscure country parish where the parishioners didn't know what the hell he was talking about— so felt he must be a Protestant or losing his faith. He died before they could find another spot for him. What they should have done was simply give him a room and books and freedom—and some day such things may come to pass. In the meantime . . ."

He ruffled the leaves of the book.

"In the celestial harmonies, which planet sings soprano, which alto, which tenor, and which bass?"

Kepler admitted that there was no relationship between human singing and the planets, but he was following it up because he was obsessed with the idea. Saturn and Jupiter were bass. Mars was tenor. Earth and Venus were alto, while Mercury was soprano. I don't remember the details but the professor expounded in obvious delight, and I missed chapel and was given three demerits.

Donovan explained that the locked cabinet in the library under the title "*Index Librorum Prohibitorum*" was a repository of forbidden books.

"Harmless, really," he said; "most of them are Dietrich's, but they're in Latin and no one around here is going to wade through them. I have Gibbon's *Decline and Fall of the Roman Empire* if you ever want to sneak in and read it. It's nonsense having it on the Index."

Here was a man, a Catholic, who was not afraid of the flames of hell for reading forbidden books. He was a man who with a boy explored knowledge in the manner of the legendary Father Dietrich.

Yet the encounters were disturbing. I was like a ferret nosing out trails and scents in the library. What I found seemed to be more and more in conflict with the simple, if fundamental, explanations of our teachers.

"How is it we're taught to believe that December 25 is Christmas, the day Jesus was born, when it isn't?"

"Whoa there, my boy," exclaimed Donovan. "It is in reality an adaptation. Christianity was in confrontation with paganism. December 25 was *dies natalis*, the birthday of the sun god, Mithras. About the fourth century, the birthday of Christ was changed from January 6 to December 25. This concerns a matter of theology. In effect, the theology of the light of Christ on the world."

He smiled at my confusion.

"The Christian missionaries adopted many things into the Christian liturgy. Baptism with salt and holy water is one. The sanctuary lamp. Now we come back to Father Dietrich. He was also deeply interested in the liturgy and how it evolved. One of his deepest differences with the-powers-that-be concerned how we should go back to simple practices—explain to the people how the Church evolved—and I daresay stop some of the present practices. Used to say there was too much pomp and incense and too little common sense."

Before I left St. Gerald's, I asked him why there was such a gap between teachers and students. He sat thinking for some time before replying.

"I think you are really groping for something else. Most of you boys who come here do so because your parents or the parish priest believe or imagine you have a vocation."

I squirmed.

"I know. I know. My old mother thought having a priest in the family was a kind of passport to heaven. I tried. Then I took what seemed second best and that didn't work. Now I have what you might call the mark of it. I believe. No matter what I may say in my strange search, I believe in the presence—but not always in the way His divine work is executed."

He paused.

"I am becoming more puzzling by the moment. Let me put it this way. A man with a jaunting car in Cork was asked how many passengers his jaunting car would carry. He said, 'If you sit contagious, it will hold four. If you sit familiar, it will hold six.'"

He paused.

"Church and school are sitting contagious, but some day it will become the other way. When we learn to sit familiar as the Church fathers and teachers did it will be an easier ride for all."

Chapter 16

INTERIM

Some of my frustration had been poured out in the Easter holidays by writing stories. I couldn't stop writing. My former schoolmates had been withdrawn, my parents were caught up in the strange troubles of the store, and my passion was for writing. I didn't know what else to do with it, but write and keep on writing.

In a desperate move I had mailed the handwritten manuscripts to editors. The names were simply copied from the magazines on the rack in a Handrich pharmacy. One came from a religious magazine Father Morrison gave me because it contained an article on vocations.

In the month after my return to St. Gerald's my mother dutifully sent me several that had been returned. Each contained printed rejection slips. Two noted in pencil that they didn't read handwritten manuscripts. She wrote wearily that she was tired of sending them back, and did I mind if she simply left them for me. There was also an accumulation of samples and magazines arriving and it was costing a lot in postage to send the stuff on to me.

I went mechanically through the college routines. Teachers complained of my daydreaming. I would come groping out of sleep several times in the night, wanting to cry out, restraining myself when I recognized the familiar dormitory. Then, one night, it was all different!

The faces around the bed were crazy, distorted, like pictures through a rain-washed window. The voices were frightening. The people were hunched and whispering, but the voices spiraled down through a well and thundered in my ears.

"Is it dangerous?"

"It has me stumped."

Pictures and blackouts alternated. The kitchen . . . outside in the crisp air that knifed in my throat . . . swimming in a cocoon of heat and sweat . . . seeing the sky with specks of light in it, and feeling the swaying cradle motion of the sleigh, and the bells that jangled loud and faded away into whispers as the scenes dimmed.

"It won't be long now. Just rest." There was the painful, dreadful frustration of trying to talk and having the words clot up in my throat. There were the times when I could hear the voices . . . near and clear in my ears . . . but no one else seemed to hear me. There was the drifting, softlike floating in tepid water, and being disturbed as they put me in a car; and the anger at having the pleasant mood shattered as the car bounced and bumped around. Then came escape into a world of warm, fleshy pink that was almost smothering.

"Will he be all right, Doctor?"

"We just have to trust in God now."

It was baffling to try and determine what God had to do with it. This was the first time I had ever had a personal contact with God, except for a private swearing session out of sight and sound of the family on the back fifty when I was trying to play grownup. When I looked up, I could imagine Him behind a cloud listening; I ran home frightened half to death. Now God was riding with me. He was looking after me. Would He remember the swearing and be so angry as to neglect me?

There were shadows in my consciousness and someone must have been behind the shadows; but it was all so elusive, and nothing would materialize except for a very ugly creature that snapped and tried to bite. It was a kind of dog or an old woman, or part of both. The familiar faces went and were replaced by disembodied ones that stood like stalks on top of swishing, white objects. At times they were gentle and at other times they tried to tear me apart. There had to be an escape, and yet there was none.

Snap was my dog and we were on the side of the grassy hill that overlooked the swale and swamp and creek. The grass was brittle, warm, and dry, and the heat poured down like liquid.

"Come on, Snap, come here now."

He wouldn't come and kept scampering just out of my reach. He couldn't or wouldn't hear me, and I wanted to cry. The tears were ice cold and rattled down my cheeks like hail that alternately burned and chilled my skin. The dead tree by the old gravel pit traced crazy, black, naked branches against the sky. When I went to lie under it, the tree wasn't a tree after all but an old woman with a tattered black dress, and she was angry—so very angry.

"Open your mouth . . . open your mouth," she screamed.

Then the voice quieted. I was aware of the room and of floating in a white bed with two nurses floating alongside. There was a strange man hovering over me.

"Take me home, Doctor, please take me home."

I was pleading, but the words were rattling around inside, and they didn't get out at all. He was smiling.

"Good boy. You had us frightened. We thought you were going." I tried to lift my hand to touch him, but my arms were lead-heavy and refused to obey.

"You hang on. The worst is over. You'll be fine now, my boy."

I was gone again, slipping back into the unreal world of shadows and memories and suddenly remembering where the toy truck was that I had lost. It was down the old well. It had fallen in, and now I wanted to go and get it but I couldn't get the top off the well. When I did pull the boards back, the black, dead water splashed up and washed me into inkiness.

I came to slowly. I was edging in from an unknown distance.

When my eyes opened, the place was semi-darkened. It was a big room with a small light at the end of a row of beds—and someone was bent over the table. I could hear noises like Grandfather breathing heavy on damp nights when his lungs rasped. A tiny bell rang. The heel taps on the floor were muffled small shots.

This was no longer a dream. My mouth was hot and dry. When I tried to move my toes, they responded, and then my knees and then my arms. I shifted in the bed and a sound escaped my lips. I saw the person move from the small table and come down the row between the beds. There was a swishing sound and a rattle of little beads like seeds in dried pods. There was a soft pressure on my forehead. I looked up to see a face wreathed in white, with the outer outlines of black, and a voice said, "Try to sip a little water."

The arm under my head was like a feather cushion. I was very tired.

"Feel better?"

I didn't have to speak. There was Otto at the foot of the bed. There were tears in his eyes.

"Hello, Harry. You're gonna get better, Harry."

I knew it, and in a vague way tried to lift my hand and wave to him. It was my first real crisis away from home. I had survived and Otto was my friend. I went into a dreamless sleep.

The college became completely unreal after I returned from the hospital. We were an island detached from the outside world. No one talked about the significance of Gandhi being released; instead we heard from Father O'Malley about the triumphs of the Church in the thirteenth century. I dimly recall hearing about Franklin D. Roosevelt, but St. Augustine seemed to be more of a living figure; one student was disgraced for asking about Martin Luther and what order he had belonged to in the Church. We shuffled through a 6 A.M. Mass and heard faintly, "*Corpus Domini nostri Jesu Christi custodiat animam tuam in vitam aeternam.*"

There was a frantic effort to produce enough saliva to swallow the Host whole without chewing.

In the evening there was Benediction. It was solemn and impressive, and to this day the Tantum Ergo sounds in my memory with a resonance that matches the glory of the eye of the great golden spikes of the eye of the monstrance. We were warned not to look at it for fear of losing our eyesight at seeing the Body of Christ.

We knew more about the Holy Land than about Canada. Father Schmidt, who had studied in Rome, taught us familiarity with the Vatican but we scarcely knew where Ottawa was, guessing it to be north of Toronto.

Fantasies poured out on paper. I lived with fantasies for real as well. A pale slim girl in town who dispersed sweet ginger ale in a lemon-colored uniform was an object of undying love. I literally drank gallons of the stuff just to be able to sneak in a few words with her.

Madame Bovary was illicit reading. It gave me an inspiration to search for camellias to send the waitress when the term was finished. It was an idle dream because my money had all been expended on ginger ale. Hearing, "Brother Can You Spare A Dime" on a prefect's crystal set struck me forcibly.

The college revue, held on the second last school day, was a major event in the school year and a magnet to me. No one would allow me to perform, so I became stage manager. Musicians (apart from a piano player, a ukulele strummer, and a terrible saxophonist) were not available. In desperation I pleaded with the rector to allow me to use his radio, a prized instrument given to him by his family on the twenty-fifth anniversary of his ordination.

I planned to turn it on at eight and the manager of the local radio station would play suitable music. The idea was electrifying. A New Gordon *Record* newspaper reporter wrote about the daring innovation. An editorial excitedly praised our ingenuity. This might change the world of theater! Radio would become an integral part of theater production! Meanwhile musicians wrote bitter letters to the newspaper denouncing us as "tools of the machine age," depriving honest workmen of their daily bread.

On the night of the performance the radio was out front on the stage to one side of the curtain. The first actor was to turn it off on the closing bars of the "Poet and Peasant Overture." This required clever co-ordination in raising the curtain.

The dean stood up at seven fifty-five, and after gazing fondly on his massive radio set, made five minutes of opening remarks. They were filled with allusions to the marriage of technique and theater. He stopped speaking at exactly eight. Otto then poked an arm out from behind the curtain and turned up the radio volume. We were dead on. The music swelled and filled the auditorium. At eight-fifteen we hauled up the curtain. Then disaster struck. The cord had been somehow placed over the lower pole of the curtain and plugged in backstage. We hauled heartily and rolled up the cord. There was a flash of sparks, a fuse blew somewhere, and all the stage lights blacked out. The radio teetered and crashed into the empty orchestra pit.

I lived in dread during the last day of school. The teacher who had encouraged me to write told me that the faculty had paid for the radio repairs. He said in a mystifying way that they were pleased to do it. The rector was still frosty with me. I wrote a story in which he was the villain, but prudently destroyed it.

I was going home with mixed feelings. A boy who had scarcely talked to me all year came wandering along to perch on my cot and watch while I clumsily packed the old trunk. There were still four hours until train time.

"Going home, eh? Where are you going?"

"Going to see my mother in New York, and she'll get tired of me in a couple of weeks and send me off to my old man in Chicago or Florida or wherever he is, and I'll end up eventually with my grandparents in Ohio."

I said lamely, "You'll be traveling, anyhow. I'll be on the farm or in the store all summer long with no place to go."

"That would be fun," he said, and got up and walked away as if there was nothing more to be said.

I stared at the white sweater with the big college letter on it and wondered about the reactions it would stir at home. I was proud to get that letter and sweater for playing rugby. I placed it at the bottom of the trunk.

"You got real animals and stuff on your farm?"

It was Timmy, the pest, an energetic little busybody with a reputation as a squealer. On this day, I welcomed him. I explained that we also had a store but he persisted in questioning me about the farm.

"Sure, all kinds of animals."

"Will you drive horses and stuff around?"

"Of course."

"It must be great. I was on a farm once. It was fun."

"Were you visiting relatives?"

"No, it was just a farm." He started away and then came back to lean closer to me.

"They took all us kids to the country one year after a big fire at the orphanage."

"Orphanage?"

"Yeh, I haven't got any relatives. I got in here on a scholarship."

"Well, what are you doing this summer?"

"I'm going to work in the office at the orphanage. Have a good summer."

I went back to hiding the objects I knew I couldn't explain at home. The photos of Red Grange and Knute Rockne stolen from the movie marquees had to be well hidden. The surreptitious notes from *La Dame aux Camélias* were a real problem.

It was time to say good-by to Otto Alberts. We had been avoiding each other. We didn't know what to say to one another.

"Packed?"

"Yeah. Don't know where the stuff comes from."

"Goin' on the train?"

"My uncle's picking me up tonight."

"Oh."

"When does your train go?"

"Three-fifteen."

"You'll be home early."

"Unhunh."

We walked over the cinders and came to the "smoking zone" behind the founder's statue. Otto grinned.

"Don't need to hide now."

"No, and now I don't feel like smoking."

"Harry," said Otto, after a long pause, "you've been awful good to me. I knew you were joshed about me being a seeing-eye mouse for you and all that. I appreciate the way you stuck up for me."

"Nobody has to stick up for you, Otto."

"It would have been a lot different if you hadn't been my friend."

"Thanks, and I'll never forget you."

"But you'll be coming back."

"No. There's no money. I hope you go on."

He walked away. I didn't call to him because he was crying. It was a relief when my trunk was taken down by the porter while I walked to the station. The rest were going on the main line and I was taking a branch line to connect with the route to our valley. It was mid-afternoon and the depot smelled of oiled floors and coal dust. Some stout women, evidently back from the market, carried empty baskets and sat in the bunched way of tired people who have to make idle conversation.

The seats in the coach were the faded green-plush kind, and the floor was dirty. It was hot inside, and when you opened the window, the air felt gritty. I was numb and amazed, in a way, that my first year of college was over, and I was going home.

It seemed strange that a feeling of exultation kept eluding me. When the train pulled into the Clover station at dusk, I saw my father waiting beside the bay window where you could make out the green shade of the lamp over the telegraph key. His hand felt rough and horny and I was aware that mine was soft. The conversation was heavy at first, and then it died down and my heart felt chilled to the point where I had to force myself to ask about the family and the business. Finally, we both gave up and rode home in the enveloping silence.

Chapter 17

FAREWELL

At first the valley and the store and the people seemed the same, but I missed the farm. It was still there but the familiar old house was boarded up. It looked sad. Weeds fringed it and sow thistles displayed enormous purple flowers in the place where my mother had cultivated a garden. Gates sagged. When I went there a band of sadness pressed around my chest.

The trouble was that while people were polite, conversations were often tinged with an edge of awkwardness, in some cases almost resentment.

"What does it feel like to have to work again?"

There was no answer to a question like that. Country people thought of work in physical terms. Work was the important thing in life. I turned to work as a defensive measure.

The baskets of eggs and the cans of cream came in Tuesday and Wednesday. The eggs had to be candled and the cream tested before shipment Thursday morning. I worked like an automaton putting the eggs up to the light and then plopping them into the crates. Extras, firsts, seconds, and occasionally murky black rots, when someone had found a hidden nest. The rots had to be handled with caution.

On Sunday morning the congregation stood around talking after Mass. Girls giggled in clusters and regarded me with curiosity. Boys I had gone to school with acted tongue-tied or else scuffed their heels in the turf and exchanged non-verbal communication that I didn't understand. It was as if the code of a secret society had been changed and no one wanted to share it with me.

I knew they headed for the swimming hole on Sunday afternoons.

"Goin' swimming this afternoon?"

Ned appeared reluctant.

"Oh, mebbe. Might just do that."

They didn't invite me. My stiff-necked pride prevented my going. Why did I expect an invitation? I probably could have gone. After the initial ragging as a form of second initiation rite, I could have been accepted.

It was Sunday. The store was closed. Father was asleep. The house was still. I tried writing, but the words would not come. I had an excuse to break my reluctance to go to the old farm. My father had mentioned something about the cattle needing a new block of salt. I caught up to Tom on the way. At the little separate school we had been close friends.

"Guess you find it pretty dull here after the city?"

"No," I replied, "I like coming home."

But the talking stalled. We tried dollops of conversation. He started talking about one of the Harley girls being caught in the hay mow with a hired hand. Tom reddened and stopped.

"Go on, tell me what happened."

"Oh, gosh, it wasn't anything."

"Old man Harley must have near killed him. He had a hell of a temper, as I remember."

"He grabbed him by—"

Tom went silent.

"What's wrong with you?"

"Oh damn, I shouldn't be telling you this anyhow."

"Why not?"

"Well, with you going through to be a priest and all—"

I could not explain because I was a marked man, and it was

indelible. We were relieved when we arrived at the gate of the farm. I took the block of salt from the barn to the pasture and stopped for a cold drink of spring water.

I lay back in the grass. Late June was all around me. The air had the natural incense that is compounded of everything from pollen to the fragrance of new-mown hay. To crush a clover stem or sniff a clover blossom was to release a heady smell.

This farm with its weather-beaten barn, showing neglect through non-tenancy, had an almost spiritual hold on me. The house, seemingly snuggled into the ground, was the place where I was born. The old back stoop was where the family sat on summer evenings and soaked up the atmosphere of cricket sounds and night noises.

This was the place of soft lamplight from the screen door where June bugs dashed themselves into dizziness. I could hear the pines softly swishing in the faintest breeze and feel the familiar fear when the bats glided around the edge of night.

I remembered the still heat of a July night when the house was smothering. We had lain out on quilts under the pine trees. It was so real I could hear Grandfather come coughing out of open-mouthed sleep exclaiming, "I'm going into the house away from those damned birds." We laughed sleep away, going back to our beds an hour before daylight when the night breezes brought feathers of coolness.

"It will rain in the morning," Father said in a resigned way, "and the oats are still not stooked in the east field."

The rain slurped down after a violent thunderstorm. I had watched him walking with sloped shoulders through the west field. The oats there had been standing and uncut and now they were a matted mass. He had spent a long time just walking around.

"Will I call him for dinner, Ma?" I asked finally.

"No, don't call him," she said gently, "he has to lose his misery first."

He did come finally and he never mentioned the ruined field.

Next morning he started to scythe it, trying to salvage as much as possible.

"It's too bad," I said, taking a pail of spring water to him in mid-morning.

He drank the water, poured the remainder on his red, polka-dotted handkerchief to mop his face.

"Could have been worse. Poor Murphy lost his whole crop."

My brother had also been born in that house. It became a place of mystery with the bent little doctor who washed his hands so carefully in the hot water and dried them on the white towels my aunt brought from the spare bedroom. He had poured something from a bottle on his hands and it reminded me of the carbolic smell I associated with sheep-shearing.

"Look in my coat pocket," he said to me.

I took out a rumpled white sack.

"You take those and run along outside." They were gum drops and I sat with my back to the pine tree and tried to make my mind go blank. I couldn't because of the noise from the upstairs bedroom, and Grandfather, who sat by the woodpile smoking his pipe, motioned for me to come with him.

We walked back the rutted laneway to the bush. It was cool among the maples. The sugar shanty was like an enchanted house in a fairy story. Birds were gossiping in the trees. When we sat on a hollow log the chipmunks came up brassily to inspect us.

The sunlight filtered in.

"It's like a church."

Grandfather had nodded. "This is what God's church is really like."

The memories faded, and when I went back to the store that Sunday my mother was at the kitchen table worrying over accounts. Father had gone away in the Model T truck.

"There are two letters here for you," my mother said absent-mindedly. "Oh, and I forgot there are some others here as well. I'm sorry but with you coming home and all I clean forgot."

I rummaged through the pile, annoyed she could have kept them for two weeks. Rejections! Printed slips. There was a letter from Otto saying he was not going back to school. There was a slim envelope from a Toronto daily newspaper I had bombarded with short-short stories. They printed one every day and my chances had seemed greater there than anywhere else.

A check for twelve dollars! Two stories accepted! This must be for every writer the supreme moment of his life. I was crying.

"Mother look—look."

She nodded.

"That's nice."

Nothing more. There was probably nothing else she could say. What did I expect? Writing was a strange and mysterious process.

I gathered up the letters. I hadn't bothered to open several because they were sample magazines or rejections. I could gauge by the size. A slim envelope with an American postmark slipped from the pile. My hands trembled. A pulp magazine had accepted "Revenge of the Hurons." Two cents a word. Thirty-seven hundred and fifty words. The check was for seventy-five dollars. The editor would be glad to see more material.

It was a story I had shown to one of the priests and he had typed it for me. At home there was just no way of explaining what it all meant to me. When my father came home he looked at the two checks and I felt a certain sadness in him. My elation was dampened. Grandfather was simply curious.

"You mean they pay you for those things? I never knew that. What do you know about Indians?"

I had to admit that I knew very little. The story had really come from George, one of the Indians who picked flax one year. George was missionary-trained and part white, and he had told me many stories.

That night, oblivious to the people in the store, I tried to write. My mind was a blank. Nothing would come. Even the sight of the checks didn't help. I had to get a typewriter somehow. The newspaper had said they preferred typed scripts.

For six dollars the Bingham undertaker sold me an old Olver typewriter with a key for each symbol. It was the beginning of my obsession, and of the continual battle about working in the store.

"At least you can do something around here. Pecking away at that thing all day."

The manuscripts went out, hastily conceived and badly written. No subject was too remote. I pored over magazines and wrote stories about places I knew only by name. They were embellished with emotions I didn't understand.

They were all returned, except for one more the newspaper accepted. Their rates had gone down to three dollars. The gap with my family widened.

"Harry," said Father Morrison, one day when he came into the store when I was alone and writing, "have you thought perhaps you need more experience. I don't know much about writing but it seems to me a person has to know a good deal before he can express himself. You should go back to college and get a good education."

He paused.

"You might think about the Jesuit order. I have never been close to the Jesuits, but they do allow their members to concentrate on special work."

"Like writing."

He sighed.

"I see a lot of books written by men with the letters S.J. after their names. I understand, some quite good books."

Father Morrison was not a reader. That didn't affect my dreaming; the aspirations had more to do with getting an opportunity to write than having a vocation.

The summer days ground on. August was hot and the farmers were busy. My father was quiet and preoccupied. You could hear the sound of the threshing machine pampaming away down the road at the Doyle place. I had been offered a day's work pitching sheaves, but hadn't gone. I suspected that my refusal to go had bothered my father. He had been fussing around the shelves where he seemed to be rearranging the same tinned goods. Finally he came to sit down near where I was typing in the alcove behind the overall counter.

"What do you plan on doing this fall?"

I was nonplused. In a summer of furious creativity I had forgotten about college. Each story I sent out seemed to open up new possibilities. When they came back, I simply mailed them on to another magazine on the list that had come from a booklet of addresses purchased for one dollar from a writer's magazine. I had no idea what type of magazine each one was since I had seen very few of them. There were constant rebuffs, but an occasional scribbled note of encouragement from a kindhearted editor rekindled my hopes and dreams.

In my heart, however, I was beginning to feel defeat.

"I don't know. I was figuring on going back to college."

My father coughed.

"Have you got enough money?"

It came out painfully. There was not enough money to pay the wholesalers' bills. The farmers' charge accounts were mounting. Produce was a glut on the market. I had about a hundred dollars and my father could give me some—but only a little—to help.

It was a black and sleepless night. Next day, my father was gone at daylight. My mother was washing in the back kitchen. My brother was with her. Hupp's Transport pulled up to unload some binder twine. There was just enough in the till to pay for it—now more and more goods came C.O.D.

Ernie Hupp was a heavy-set man with a red face. He sat on the edge of the pile of binder twine sacks and drank a bottle of cream soda.

"Ernie, will you give me a job?"

He looked me over.

"Work is hard to get. Things are just not good. I don't know, but I guess things aren't too good for you here. None of my business but—you don't seem cut out for—oh, I was just rambling."

My heart was like a lump.

"Can't pay you much, but if you want to work nights checking and loading at the London warehouse I can give you something to live on and a place to sleep. You'll have to work with Bert."

The last part of his statement must have been a warning, but I didn't stop to think. Shirts, a pair of pants, manuscripts, and the old typewriter were dumped in the space behind the hard seats in the Mack truck. I went to the back door of the store which led into the living quarters, and couldn't force myself to open it. I didn't want to try and explain to my mother. I knew that I couldn't.

On the spike where the day's bills were put for entering in the ledgers, I stuck a note written on a piece of brown wrapping paper torn from the roll at the end of the counter.

Dear Folks: I am going away for a time to work and get enough money to go to college. I'll write as soon as possible.

That night I was on the London transport loading-dock with Bert. I had a cot in a room I shared with him next to the office. It had a hot plate, a table, a few dirty dishes, some canned goods, and a box of empty bottles. Bert, a lean wraith whose chest shrunk concavely from the bib of his overalls, showed me invoices and route lists. The empty trucks had to be loaded overnight with the cases, barrels, and bags and boxes which had been picked up during the day from the wholesalers.

Bert's bald head was wreathed with stiff gray hair. His face was red, but after several hours of exertion and frequent trips to our room it tinged toward purple. He spoke very little and frightened me in a way.

By four o'clock in the morning the trucks were loaded and we went back to the room. He made me a cup of tea and heated a can of pork and beans. He didn't eat but took pulls at a bottle of rum.

"What do you do with that thing?" he inquired, stumbling over my oversize typewriter.

"I write stories."

"Have any published?"

"Four."

"Well, well—"

He was silent for a long time.

"It's a noble thing," he said finally, and there was not a trace of sarcasm in his voice. "I once wrote. I was a newspaperman and a writer but things—troubles interfered. Let each become all that he was created capable of being; expand, if possible, to his full growth; resisting all impediments, casting off all foreign, especially all noxious adhesions, and show himself at length in his own shape and stature, be these what they may."

He rummaged under his cot, among what seemed to be a pile of books, and finally came up with a volume. It was dog-eared. He tossed it to me as he half collapsed on his cot.

"Carlyle. Have you read Macaulay? We must talk about it. Must talk about many things, my boy. I can no longer write but I am a good teacher—"

He was lying down.

"Samuel Johnson—must read him. Nobody can write—write— the life of a man but those who have eaten and drunk and lived in social intercourse with him. That's Johnson. My boy, I am glad you are here."

He was snoring in a few minutes. I approached my cot apprehensively but I was too tired to bother taking off my clothes. I slept. In fact, I slept so well I scarcely heard the trucks taking off from the warehouse. When I woke, it was eleven o'clock and a coffeepot was bubbling on the hot plate.

Bert was at the window. When the springs of my cot protested, he turned with a book in his hand.

"Listen to this, my boy. Listen—

" 'Now sleeps the crimson petal, now the white;
Nor comes the cypress in the palace walk;
Nor winks the gold fin in the porphyry font;
The firefly wakens; waken those with me.' "

He peered at me, as if waiting for a reaction. I was too tired.

"That's Tennyson. Now, my boy, if you are going to be a writer, you have to read. I've got some stories by Sherwood Anderson. And we have to talk. We can talk while we're loading. Later I find I don't concentrate too well. You have to read and write in the day. There's coffee on the stove. That diner over there will give you a hell of a breakfast for two bits. Oatmeal, eggs, ham, potatoes—the works. Rosie likes red hair."

He read on while I sipped the blackest, strongest coffee I had ever tasted. Bert had welcomed me into the world of experience. I sensed it would not be the one that Father Morrison talked about.

I didn't think of St. Gerald's. Strangely enough, before going to sleep I thought about Clover and the store and my family, not in a lonely way, but with detachment. It was something I would carry always. For if St. Gerald's had been a sanctuary on a long journey, Clover had been my true point of departure, and I would remember it clearly even if I knew I could never go back, no matter what happened.